LIGHT

MAGIC

— *for* —

DARK TIMES

Inspiring | Educating | Creating | Entertaining

Brimming with creative inspiration, how-to projects, and useful information to enrich your everyday life, Quarto Knows is a favorite destination for those pursuing their interests and passions. Visit our site and dig deeper with our books into your area of interest: Quarto Creates, Quarto Cooks, Quarto Homes, Quarto Lives, Quarto Drives, Quarto Explores, Quarto Gifts, or Quarto Kids.

22 21 20 19 18   1 2 3 4 5

ISBN: 978-1-59233-853-5

Digital edition published in 2018
eISBN: 978-1-63159-587-5

Library of Congress Cataloging-in-Publication Data available.

Design and Page Layout: Tanya Naylor, tanyasoffice.com
Illustration: Ada Keesler, @adagracee, except page 147 Lisa Marie Basile

Printed in China

100 Spells, Rituals, & Practices
for Coping in a Crisis

LIGHT
MAGIC
—— *for* ——
DARK TIMES

LISA MARIE BASILE
Foreword by Kristen J. Sollée

Caring for myself is
not self-indulgence,
it is self-preservation,
and that is an act of
political warfare.

– AUDRE LORDE, *A Burst of Light*

CONTENTS

Foreword

by Kristen J. Sollée, author of *Witches, Sluts, Feminists*

For centuries, witches and women have both thrived and suffered in the dark. They have gathered under blackened skies to commune, to study, to heal, and to practice forbidden rites in covens and consciousness-raising groups. They have found safety and solace in the shadows with one another. But because the punishing patriarchal forces that have dominated human history fear the shadows, they have also been cast as darkness itself, only to be murdered, ostracized, and abused for it.

This ambivalent relationship with darkness is one that witches, women, and all those who are part of marginalized groups share. And this ambivalent relationship with darkness is one that Lisa Marie Basile honors in *Light Magic for Dark Times*.

Like so many others, I, too, have both thrived and suffered in the dark. I have wrapped myself in funereal garb, frequented cemeteries, painted my lips and eyes black, and tattooed skulls and death sigils across my body. I have submerged myself in music and art and literature that celebrates despair and macabre mysteries. I have felt safest in the eldritch womb of the woods, the blacklight of the club.

I was drawn to the dark, on the one hand, because I didn't buy the lie that darkness was evil or wrong as my upbringing might have me believe. But, on the other hand, I knew darkness could also be the perfect hiding place. An excuse not to shed light on the trauma that pricked my insides. I endured abusive relationships in secrecy as I wore a sunny mask to the world because I was ashamed to admit what I did to try to bask in love's light. I kept my chronic illness from family and friends because I was afraid to have them associate my presence with doom and decay.

Thankfully, witchcraft was my way out of this darkness.

Light Magic for Dark Times is a book I wish I had by my bedside and in my heart during my most challenging moments. It holds space for healing and exploring and awakening the parts of ourselves that we or the outside world might label dark, and offers rejuvenating rites of lightness and illumination. Basile's spellcraft radiates love and sex-positivity, but it is certainly not hex-negative. She elevates shadow work and emphasizes the importance of delving into the dark and facing pain head-on to heal. There is no trauma too deep or desire too superficial for the spells, incantations, and rituals contained in this grimoire.

When I was writing *Witches, Sluts, Feminists: Conjuring the Sex Positive*, a sex-positive feminist primer on the witch in history and popular culture, my goal was to pay tribute to voices that have been silenced and the artists and activists who for centuries have endeavored to amplify those voices. Basile has created a practical toolkit for contemporary artists and activists of this ilk, with a whole swath of spells specifically designed for folks involved in social justice movements.

"Witchcraft has long been a tool for the oppressed to use to achieve autonomy and receive divine guidance," Basile asserts in the introduction. "And part of honing that power for yourself is fighting for the rights of others."

The conscious magic offered within *Light Magic for Dark Times* is indicative of the kind of witchcraft I see taking hold across the country. In my college classroom and in the schools I have visited to lecture about the legacy of the witch, I have found that students are just as hungry to create social justice sigils as they are to talk about the otherworldly women and witchy femmes that have seduced the cultural imagination. Yes, they still want to dress like they're in *The Craft* or *American Horror Story: Coven*, but they are equally interested in learning about witchcraft as a method of collective political action and communal self-care. They want to cloak themselves in darkness as they shine a light on the world's wounds. To these students and so many more folks outside the classroom and in the streets, casting spells is synonymous with crafting protest chants. Personal witchcraft is now, more than ever, political witchcraft.

Although there are countless injustices and horrors in the world today, I don't believe we are living in dark times that are any different than the myriad dark times of the past. However, what is different is how we relate to that darkness, how we define that darkness, and how we let it define us. With the proliferation of witchcraft manuals and magical manifestos and art of all genres that allow us to see beyond the binary of dark/light, we are poised to embrace the contradictions and complexities that populate the mercurial cultural topography we are living on. And that is why a book like this is so vital now—not because these dark times are any different, but because *we* are different, and our light is being calibrated to shine in transformative new ways.

Let *Light Magic for Dark Times* be a catalyst for your conjuring, in darkness and in light, in these times and in times to come. It certainly will be for me.

Preface

Dear reader, I imagine that in picking up this book you're ready to try something new. Maybe you've got a deep hunger to get back to your self; maybe you feel a risk must be taken. Maybe you want to create healing, autonomy, and joy out of pain or fear. With this grimoire as a guide, you can find a path through the darkness, make friends with the shadows, and conjure *sustainable* inner light. In a way that feels right to *you*.

I have always found it risky to blossom—it takes time and work, and the process of shedding our skin is uncomfortable. But as they say, if it doesn't challenge you, there's no way it can change you. Magic does both. I believe that magic—that electric force within us and nature and the cosmos—can help us create a life that is nourishing and resilient.

This magic, this space of light, dark, and shadow, grounds my life, and I work with it daily. Five years ago, I founded *Luna Luna*, a witchy, intersectional digital magazine with stories that tackle the darkness, art that conjures the light, and work that straddles the threshold. *Elle* magazine recently featured us in their "Season of the Witch" feature, and BuzzFeed called us a "girl squad you need to know."

My work as a writer and editor has always been, even before I was aware of it, informed by my magical lifestyle; I've practiced since my teen years. I'm also a poet, and in all of my collections, I've focused on the same themes: wading through the fog to find some glimmering ember, some clarity, some magical connective tissue.

> And the day came when the risk to remain tight in a bud was more painful than the risk it took to blossom.

— ANAÏS NIN

So how did I come to spell-casting and ritual? As a Scorpio (chronically Scorpio, that is), magic has always felt natural to me. I loved practices that gave me a sense of empowerment, like I could conquer (or, more accurately, learn to work with) darkness. I also had parents who encouraged my education, curiosity, and interest in magical practices. And it was this sense of magical empowerment I would lean into as I grew up.

But at the age of fifteen, I was put into foster care. It was the hardest and loneliest thing I've ever dealt with, but in many ways I'm grateful for it. It's given me resiliency and empathy, and it forced me to get creative and find autonomy in healing, dealing with pain and loss, and finding inner strength.

When I began studying magic, I took comfort in the labyrinthine musty aisles at the local library, where I devoured books about philosophy, mysticism, and witchcraft. I'd find myself meditating, calling on the elements, or mouthing incantations when I was sad or uncertain. This sort of inner magic helped save my life.

Although throughout my teens I found myself questioning my religious and spiritual beliefs (I called myself everything from atheist to agnostic to spiritual to a witch and then back again), that sense of inner magic stayed with me. I had a distinct feeling that magic came from inside of *me*, but it was also in nature and in the cosmos—and that I could commune with it by sitting in the grass, swimming in the ocean, and running through the woods. (Let's just say I got a *lot* of poison ivy!)

It felt right to light a candle and focus on a wish or dream. It felt, in many ways, formal, serious, comforting. I often cast spells so that my family would get back together. And I'd be lying if I didn't admit that I tried the stuff you see in movies, like trying to turn my eyes from brown to blue.

I was, for all intents and purposes, a teenage witch, although I didn't always call myself one. I didn't realize you could simply be a witch without being initiated or having gone through years of study. (Hint: You can.) I wish at that time that I had known others who also practiced magic.

All these years later, *Luna Luna* is a sort of magical home to me. It is a complementary platform to all the amazing historical and academic witchy literature that already exists. *Luna Luna* features essays and spells by everyday people, modern witches, and practicing beginners, and it provides a space where women and femmes can talk about why they approach tarot in a certain way or how DIY witchcraft is empowering to them.

In the *Luna Luna* community and beyond, people want to be heard, be seen, have autonomy, love and be loved, soothe pain, find inspiration, and follow the light. I hope that this book helps you achieve these things—even if it means stepping out of your comfort zone or walking into the depths of the shadow.

INTRODUCTION

———

Light Magic for Dark Times is an everyday, no-bullshit grimoire of self-care and coping practices—inspired by witchcraft to help you invoke your own personal magic.

If you've ever felt a bit different, like an unnamable, splendid energy lives within you, this book is for you. It's for you if you're interested in soul-replenishing self-care rituals. It's for you if you seek a sense of control and autonomy, whatever your circumstances. It's for you if you want to let loose and make some damn magic by the light of the moon. You'll also learn how to color outside the lines in the most productive way possible. Dreamers, thinkers, darklings, light-seekers, shadow-dwellers, rebels, and witches—welcome. By integrating magic into your lifestyle, you join a legacy of individuality, bravery, and resistance.

First things first: Your magic already exists within you; this book helps you harness those splendid feelings and energies. Maybe you're holding this book because you already use magic. Perhaps you're an atheist or an agonostic, but you love the idea of ritualizing your self-care regimen. Or maybe you're looking to augment your spiritual or wellness practices. Whoever you are, this book will help you find a balance between the light and the dark—and make it work for you.

Within these pages, you'll encounter everything from love and grief to regeneration and shadow play. These practices and routines can help when self-doubt sirens sing you their pesky songs, when political turmoil sends you into a helpless frenzy, or when you lose someone you love and become a walking wound. Whatever the ailment or desire, these spells, rituals, and practices are easy, inexpensive, and rooted in your intention. You'll also learn a bit about crystals, sigils, and herbs along the way.

Although these spells, rituals, and practices can be used by everyone, I dedicate this book to women, femmes, and anyone who has been systematically marginalized or silenced. Witchcraft has long been a tool for the oppressed to use to achieve autonomy and receive divine guidance, and I want to recognize that.

You won't find spells that require super-expensive or hard-to-find tools, and there are no rituals designed to make you skinny, pretty, or desired by men. Instead, these pages, without platitudes or false promises, offer ways to fill you with shimmering empowerment and honesty, so that you can live an authentic and high-vibe life. Sometimes, you'll be guided through the darkness to get to the light. Together, we'll lean into the process of connecting your everyday life with your inner magic, especially during rough times.

What This Book Isn't

This is not a comprehensive instructional guide to magic or witchcraft. It's not a look at the global history of witchcraft or the many kinds of magic in practice. This book isn't specifically for witches, either. In fact, it's for everyone—especially those of you who like the idea of your self-care with a heavy helping of magic. To learn more about the history of witchcraft, I encourage you to check out the resources guide at the end of this book, which will direct you to some oh-so-magical instructive books, podcasts, and websites.

You're Already Casting Spells

If you're not sure about using magic, consider this: You might already be doing it in some way—like when you come home, throw yourself into a warm, candlelit bathtub, and read something mundane enough to make you fall into a soft slumber. That's a ritual. Or when you whisper "You can do this" to yourself when you're intimidated. That's an incantation. You don't need to follow any specific religion or spiritual practice to use this book—you just need to believe in your own power.

Let's light it up.

Practicing Magic in the Modern World

All things witchy are "in" right now. You can probably find magical lifestyle books at your local clothing boutique or moon-charged oils at major retailers. The use of nature and intuition and intention (a.k.a. magic) is part of the incredible and enduring lifeblood and fabric of humanity. Today's practitioners are simply finding adaptations to the ancient Egyptians' use of amulets or the Celts' deep worship of nature.

Especially in the Western world, modern witchcraft is closely tied to social justice. Witches (usually women, the oppressed, or the poor) have existed at the fringes; many were punished for their power or forced to give up their beliefs. To adopt the practices of magic and witchery is to recognize that legacy today. And part of honing that power for yourself is fighting for the rights of others.

That being said, many people hold mixed views on witchcraft becoming "trendy"— especially those whose meaningful, lifelong practices have been appropriated for a trendy lifestyle. And many people are still unable to practice openly for fear of social or political danger or repercussions. In short, practicing magic should be considered an ethical act—it's about being aware and respecting yourself, others, and nature. The more empathy you have, the more powerful you become.

Despite the evolution of ancient practices, some people view magic as evil or Satanic or whatever else they feel like dreaming up. This view is often not based in reason, not based on research, and not formed from talking to those who practice it. Miseducation, long-held social stigma, and sexism still play a role in the way magical practices are perceived. It's important to be aware of the risks and stigmas attached to witchcraft, and make safety a top priority in your practice.

Who Is a Witch?

The better question is, who isn't?

A lot of the time, pop culture narratives depict witchcraft in limited ways. Pop culture often makes it seem like a practice performed by mostly straight white women in the Western world. And they're typically either glamorous (the fair maiden, with her long golden hair, casting sweet love spells) or they're ugly, cackling hermits (cue the crone with nose warts, consumed with exacting an evil plot, toiling over a green, goo-filled cauldron).

We're also fed the idea that a witch must be initiated by an elder or a coven, and that spells are about instant gratification (changing our hair color, meeting our one true love). None of this is entirely real. Anyone can make magic—as a solitary practitioner or in a group—and witchcraft is much more nuanced and diverse than any pop-culture depiction suggests.

Witchcraft and Self-Care

Witchcraft is a way of connecting with the world around you—to nature, to the cosmos, to your own higher self, to the *great big*-ness that exists outside of you, whether that's god or energy or any force you believe in—and a way of manipulating that energy. The witch as a symbol, as well as the practice of magic, gives us the power to assert ourselves, reclaim and grow our autonomy, and focus our energy in times of joy—and chaos.

I wrote this book with all of that in mind—because we all could use more self-care tools. As you progress through this book, you will be prompted with questions to get you to think and focus, such as:

- What are your dreams in the short and long term?
- What memories haunt you?

- What do you love about yourself?
- What is your place in the cosmos?
- What sort of role can your magic play in your community?

I hope the process of answering these questions will help you create more light during dark times.

Making Magic and Performing Witchery

Magic is many things: It's emotional, intuitive, sensual, empowering, and natural—so have fun with it, and make it your own.

First off, you don't need to be a witch to explore this book or make magic. Identifying as a witch means vastly different things to different people, and that's why the witch is such an enduring figure worldwide.

Not all witches cast spells, and not every person who casts spells is a witch. Despite what some folks might tell you, there is no one right way to be a witch, to cast a spell, or to find empowerment in ritual; our diverse cultures, backgrounds, beliefs, and values inform our magical practices. At the same time, be careful not to appropriate your magical acts or words from closed cultures. Recognizing what is or is not available to you is part of being an ethical practitioner. By doing some research, asking questions, listening carefully, and being open-minded about undoing learned appropriative behaviors, you can ensure that your craft is ethical and intersectional.

Magic Is Intuitive and Personal

Some practitioners of witchcraft prefer highly-structured ceremonies with specific ingredients and tools (think: fresh lavender, swimming in the sea during a full moon). For others (like me) it's all about setting clear intentions, playing with your inherent creativity, and using what's available to you—because we are busy, modern witches!

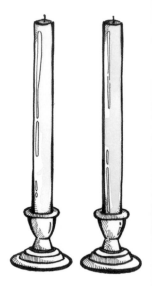

I generally consider myself secular; I don't believe in gods or goddesses or angels. Lots of other practitioners do. If you do, you should feel the freedom to incorporate those beliefs into the practices I've included here. You can do so by calling on those entities during your spells and rituals.

Tweaking magical practices to fit your emotional, religious, and logistical needs—as well as your wallet!—makes for powerful results. If you are casting a spell while thinking, "I don't associate power with this candle color," change it. If you can't afford to buy crystals or certain ingredients, swap them for another material you have on hand. You can be both intentional and practical.

The way you practice will evolve over time. The spectrum of magical practices and perspectives is as varied as the color spectrum. You may hear others say they practice folk magic or claim that they're a sea witch or a Wiccan, and that's wonderful. There's no one way of making magic or of being a witch.

That goes for baneful magic as well. You'll find no hex-shaming in this book. (Some think these sorts of spells are bad news—and that's okay, too.) Everyone has the right to practice in their own way, and it's important to respect that many traditions and cultures have their own views and reasons for hexes and cursing. Also: Sometimes a hex can help us move forward. (Just saying, darklings. I'm a Scorpio—if you cross my path, well . . .)

Rituals and Spells

Rituals and spells provide the structure and space to focus and direct energy. You can think of them as your very own conduit. But spell-casting isn't like it's portrayed in the movies. It doesn't work instantly; there's no grand finale or great gusts of wind that accompany their power. Rituals and spells are ways of fertilizing a wish or vision before you send it into the universe to be birthed. It's a germination.

I like to think of spellcraft as a kind of poetry. A poem is deeply personal, an amulet of written power. It defies the exclusive barriers of grammar and cuts straight to the core. It's a hyper-focused look at a moment, feeling, or desire.

Likewise, a spell is a condensed way of focusing your energy and intent to create something or open up the channels of receptivity. It's an individual moment of self-charged power and truth. And each spell is unique.

Using Your Intention

Intention is the core ingredient of magic. Think of intention as the gas for your magical car. It's the rose's red color. It's that lingering, powerful base note (musk? cedar?) in your night-out perfume. It's the quiet, humming electricity of actualization.

That doesn't mean you can simply make a wish for a million dollars or cure cancer or stop crime, though. (Oh my darling, I wish we could.) This is because, in many ways, you can only work with what's already there or has the potential to be there. So if finding a million dollars or stopping crime isn't probable right now, it's not likely to happen.

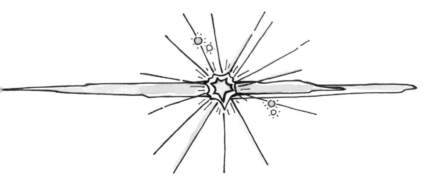

Magic can do a lot for you, though. It can help you gaze into the mirror of self-truth, put dark thoughts to bed, and help you make real time for self-care. A wish for money might translate to a spell to help you be receptive to new opportunities, and a spell for love might help you focus on—and project—what (or who) you want to attract.

That said, some people have the idea that our own mind-sets are to blame for our misfortune or ill health. You may hear terms like "poverty mind-set" or "low-vibe life." This sort of thinking might find its roots in a grossly privileged misunderstanding of the Law of Attraction, which suggests that what we put out into the world we get back. That's true to some extent, but if you're born into poverty and face social barriers because of it, your mind-set isn't to blame. If you're cruel to others and get cruelty in return, that's one thing. But you're not responsible for the systemic obstacles set up against you.

You might not find that you've put an end to all acts of classism or oppression by performing certain practices or rituals, but you will find that you have more strength, clarity of mind, and compassion to be able to achieve a sense of balance. And this, in turn, might help you make lasting personal or social change. Intention is a powerful thing.

It is not always easy to focus on our intentions, however. In fact, it's a privilege we don't all have. Our focus has to compete with long work hours, family demands, health conditions, and social justice issues, just to name a few. With this book, my intent is that you'll take a few moments for you—to heal, to explore, to create, to reflect, and to play—especially when times are chaotic and dark.

Some of this book may even require you to dive into the abyss to come out on the other side. My goal isn't to placate you with squeaky-clean faux positivity (and even if I tried to, I'm more Wednesday Addams than peppy cheerleader). Instead, I aim to help you find small, realistic ways to gain strength, autonomy, and joy.

When you're working with the spells, rituals, and practices in this book, you are the one in charge, on your own timeline. I've provided prompts, but your interpretation is the final word. You don't need to do everything my way. Many witches—especially in the modern era—find power in customizing their magic and doing bits of this and that. Magic, dear darkling, can work only if you get behind it.

Pre-Magic Prep

You may have some burning questions by now—and that's natural. You're about to embark on a journey that requires you to focus and go deep, so I want to clarify some ideas around magic and this book while also sharing with you some techniques and tricks to use before you get started.

Magical F.A.Q.s

Before you begin reading the spells in the chapters ahead, I want to share answers to some questions that may provide clarity around witchery and a general foundation for your spell-casting and ritualizing.

Is Witchcraft a Religion?

While it may seem so, witchcraft is not a religion. There's no one god or goddess, and there are many (nearly endless) ways that one might practice it. Witchcraft is more of a lifestyle—one that values nature and a connection to the vastness of our world and the cosmos beyond it. Many witches do meld their practice with more organized religious beliefs, while others don't. And others are atheists. Everyone is on a different path.

What If I Don't Have One of the Tools in This Book?

You're welcome to remove items, cut steps, or skip from page to page. This is all about your intentions, goals, and healing.

What Is the Difference Between a Spell, a Ritual, and a Practice?

For the purposes of this book, these terms are used somewhat interchangeably. A ritual can contain a spell, and a spell can also be a sort of magical practice. In this book, a spell tends to incorporate a goal or an incantation (a spoken magical phrase); a ritual tends to include a repetitive act; and a practice is usually an activity without any formal structure or spell component. Feel free to fold certain aspects of one into another—be creative and build on what feels right to you.

REQUIRED MATERIALS

Here are all the materials you will come across in this book.
(Remember: Substitutes are totally fine!)

- Pen
- Paper
- Journals for writing practices and for shadow work
- Crystals
    - Rose quartz
    - Shadow quartz
    - Obsidian
    - Amethyst
    - Clear quartz
- Candles (various colors, including white, black, pink, and gray)
- Black yarn
- Salt
- Tea (lavender)
- Sachet bags or zip-lock bags
- Spray bottle
- Fireproof bowl
- Lighter
- Candle snuffer
- Lipstick or chapstick

Do I Need to Believe in God or a Higher Power to Use This Book?

No. You'll use your own energies to effect change.

I've Heard I Shouldn't Blow Out My Candles After Casting a Spell—Is This True?

Many witches believe it's bad luck or bad form to blow out a candle after a spell. Instead, you may use a snuffer or a fan. That said, if you really need to blow out a candle for whatever reason, do it—especially if it means stopping a fire risk! Generally speaking, fire's pretty cool—until it burns down your house. Some other candle tips: Light candles with another candle when you can. Also, spells tend to work best when you're using a new candle. Old energy can "stick" to them.

Always burn candles safely and in a safe environment. You know: No painting your nails and then lighting up. No going to sleep with candles burning. Make sure your pets won't get burned or knock over your lit candles. And always burn paper and other things in fireproof bowls near or in a sink.

Can a Magical Lifestyle Fix All My Problems?

I wish. This book should be used as one tool in your wellness arsenal—but it's not the only tool. This book is not a replacement for professional health care or mental health care. You deserve love, care, and help when you need it.

What about Crystals?

Throughout this book, you may be asked to use a crystal for a certain spell. I've used crystals you can generally find at esoteric bookstores, occult shops, and Etsy shops, rather than hard-to-find ones you'll need to hunt for. Most of these crystals can be found at low cost.

But it's all right if you don't have the specific crystal on hand for most of these. For the spells in this book, crystals can boost your magical practice by representing love, strength, or healing, for example. Many people like to make up their own crystal associations.

Should I Use Medicinal Plants, Herbs, and Flowers?

Never ingest anything without knowing if it's safe for you to do so. Certain herbs contraindicate medicines, while others may trigger an allergy. If you do use plants, get them from trusted sources. Plucking them from a garden sounds magical, I know, but it could be risky (or illegal).

How Do I Manifest Like the Witch I Am?

One of the best ways to manifest is to believe your goal has already happened. Meditate, visualize, and set intentions. Writing goals or dreams in the present, rather than the future, is one potent way of manifestation.

Can Spells Control or Change Another Person?

Changing someone's will is often considered unethical or pointless; people are who they are. Though movies and books have long promoted the idea that you can simply cast a spell on someone to make them love you or give up a bad habit, many witches stick with the idea that this is not only unethical but also a waste of energy because magic usually works with what's already there. I have included spells, rituals, and practices that acknowledge the autonomy of others.

How Do I Prepare My Mind, Body, and Space for These Spells, Rituals, and Practices?

Grounding is the act of centering yourself in your body in the here and now. Taking the time to do this before some magical practices can help you clear your mind and focus your energy without feeling pulled in a million directions. No one is perfect—drifting thoughts and feelings are bound to cross your mind while performing magic. But grounding beforehand will help you stay more firmly rooted in the moment and in your power.

If you think of magic as the paint, then grounding is the canvas, as it preps everything. This doesn't mean work without grounding is for naught—magic works if you put energy behind it. Grounding just means you can focus more easily. Some forms of magic don't need it. Sex magic, for example, works off your sexual energy—not your grounded energy. You get to choose when you want to use this tool.

TECHNIQUES FOR GROUNDING

· Sit or stand with your palms open. Imagine your spinal cord flowing into the earth, rooting with it deep down below. Feel the negative energy flowing out and dissipating, and feel clarity and calm grow beneath you.

· Take several deep belly breaths, envisioning anything toxic and problematic exhaling with your breath.

· Stand outside and take your shoes off. Connect with the earth and feel its natural, splendid energy wash over you.

· Taking care of yourself is a form of grounding, so you may want to go for a run or stretch before spell-casting. Drinking a glass of water helps, too, since water purifies and cleanses our bodies. A magic-maker can never be too hydrated.

Cleansing

Cleansing is useful when casting a spell or making sure an object like a crystal doesn't contain old, potentially negative energies. Basically, the space where you're spell-casting or meditating should be prepped for magic. It can be hard to relax in a messy room, right? The same is true in magic—especially if you performed a particularly heavy ritual or used a crystal to absorb seriously dark energy. Plus, the symbolic act of cleansing your space can help you get into the mind-set of magic. And mind-set is our number one tool.

CLEANSE YOUR SPACE OR BELONGINGS

- Close your eyes and envision the space clear of all harmful, chaotic, or negative energies.
- Fill a simple spray bottle with water. (You can add a few drops of essential oil or some herbs.)
- Many practitioners burn palo santo, cedar, or sage for a smoke cleanse. Many other traditional herbs will work, too. Please don't perform a smoke cleanse in rooms or homes where little animals, children, or babies live. And please check with roommates first.
- Salt can cleanse objects like crystals (but be sure to first check that the salt doesn't harm your type of crystal). For this cleansing technique, you want to submerge the object in salt.
- Moonlight and sunlight can cleanse objects.

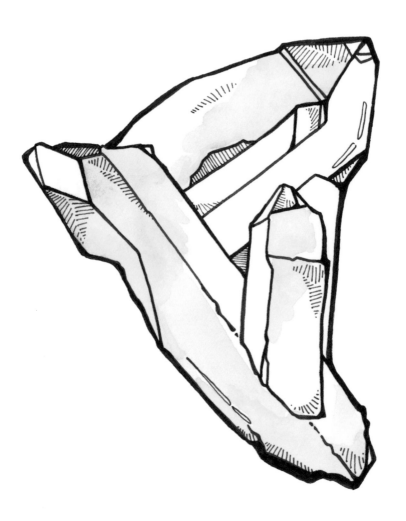

LOVE

———

Receiving and Conjuring
Adoration for Yourself
and Others

1

The phrase "love spell" conjures images of crushes finally falling to their knees in blubbering adoration, rose petals, bubbling elixirs, and happily-ever-afters. And although I've included a spell here for anyone who is seeking their one true love, there is a caveat: Magic can open the doors of receptivity, and it can widen the threshold between present and possibility, but it should not be used to force someone into loving you. For one, consent is super sexy. And second, the universe—in all its mystery—knows who and what is best for you. Magic helps you align with that universal energy, and pull it in nice and close.

> As a sweet apple reddens on top of a tree, on top of the topmost bough, that pickers have missed—no, not really missed, but could not reach . . .

– SAPPHO

LIGHT MAGIC for DARK TIMES

But love is about so much more than all of that. It's about the way we feel toward ourselves, how we treat the people around us, and what we do to care for others.

Just as Sappho—a seventh-century classical Greek poet, and one of the few well-known lady poets at that time—wrote at the beginning of this chapter, sometimes love can seem elusive.

While that may apply to romantic love, it also applies to the love we feel toward ourselves. In an age where we are regularly fed messages about what makes us worthy, beautiful, and desirable, it's hard to untangle our self-image from the chaos.

In this chapter, I ask that, like Sappho, you undress your vulnerabilities and ask yourself the hard questions:

- What do I love about myself?
- Why do I find it hard to feel self-love?
- How can I send love to others?
- Who needs compassion, empathy, and support?
- How can I show my body more love?
- What is it about being alone that scares me?
- What makes me goddamn delicious?

When dealing with matters of love, there are so many factors: self-esteem, willingness to accept others' feelings for you, willingness to give love. As you move through the spells, rituals, and practices in this chapter, I hope you'll meditate on these questions and come to a deeper understanding of yourself. I also hope you'll find that self-care is an act of love that benefits not only you but also the people you interact with.

A Spell for Sending Supportive Love to Someone Facing Hardship

When someone you know could use a dose of love and support, it can be difficult to know just how to do that. Words can sound like empty platitudes, while saying nothing can feel just as wrong. You can let them know you love and support them, but this spell acts as a sort of signal boost—helping the people or person know that you care.

Materials

Rose quartz (or other symbol of love)

Candle

Picture of the person/people or a paper with their names

Hold your rose quartz in one hand. Light your candle and lay the picture or paper with the name of the person alongside it. Think about their face, their essence, and their words, and meditate on what you think they must be feeling. Are they sad? Have they experienced a trauma? Think about those feelings and empathize with their situation. Imagine your love and compassion filling the quartz—and when you feel like you've sufficiently filled the crystal, place it on the paper or photograph. Hold your hand atop the crystal, feeling the energy build between you, the crystal, and the person you're sending love to.

Snuff out the candle only when you're confident you've sent the message.

Keep the photograph or piece of paper with the person's name on your bedside table, underneath the crystal, for the next three days.

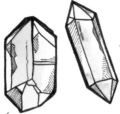

MAGICAL CRYSTALS

For centuries, crystals have been used by cultures throughout the world for healing, even dating back to the ancient Egyptian pharaohs. And today, more and more people are using crystals in their everyday wellness practices, as amulets of power, meditative tools, and decorations of natural splendor.

According to Judy Hall, a leading authority on crystals and stones, they contain stable energy and frequencies that we can use in our magical practices (and even in everyday devices like watches and computers). Their shapes and colors have special significance when used in magical practice, but you may find that a particular crystal feels one way to you and not the same for someone else. Honor that.

Popular crystals and stones include:

Rose quartz: Love, compassion, positivity, harmony

Amber: Cleansing, energy, clarity

Amethyst: Dream recollection, healing, tranquilizing, meditative

Turquoise: Protective, strengthening, inner calm

Shungite: Healing the body, breaking bad habits

Kunzite: Happiness, high vibes, healing

Quartz: Cleansing, recalibrating, balancing, healing

Obsidian: Protection, negativity removal, centering, severing ties

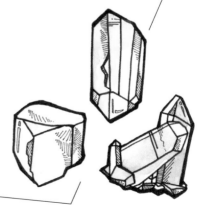

A Self-Love Ritual for Tapping into Your Body After a Long Day

When you've had one of those defeating, endless, energy-sucking days, all you want to do is get out of your head. No more emails, no more ideas, no more communication. And one of the best ways to get out of your head is to get into your body. This practice can be done anytime you want to destress and connect with your flesh and blood, and it works wonderfully before bed. This spell is best done when you're alone, so you can focus on you.

Materials

Your bathroom shower

Lingerie or cozy pajamas

Red candle

Small pinch of cinnamon

Your favorite body oil or lotion

Your favorite perfume

Take a shower, envisioning the day's stress slipping off of your skin and down the drain. When you're done, after you've dried off, get into whatever you've chosen to wear. Head to your bedroom (or wherever you'd like to perform this ritual) and light your candle.

Say aloud:

This candle of my body,
alight, of fire.
This cinnamon,
a devotion, at the altar of myself.
In sleep, I become a garden of roses
blooming in the dark.

Mix the cinnamon into your oil or lotion and smooth it over your body, paying careful attention to each of your beautiful body parts. (Skip this step if you're allergic to cinnamon or if you have sensitive skin.) Revel in yourself. Cinnamon is said to evoke sensuality, love, and energy, so it's good to use in a restorative practice. Spray your favorite perfume and bask in its scent: What are the notes? How do they smell on your warm skin? What does it make you feel? One of my favorites is a musky rose—it's light and clean, and it reminds me of fresh, floral linens. It helps me fall into a calm space.

Next, get comfortable on the bed. Close your eyes and focus on each body part—from your feet to your scalp. Breathe in and out deeply, focusing on the rhythm of your breath. Imagine warm, deep-red light glittering over your skin, body part by body part. Pay special attention to your curves, your shapes, your hair, and any body part that needs extra love. Bask in your beauty and gently run your hands over your skin. Stay in this space, preferably going to bed after you've completed this practice. (Just make sure you blow out the candle!)

One of the best ways
to get out of your head
is to get into your body.

A Pick-Me-Up Rose-Quartz Elixir for Self-Love

It's normal to feel insecure, unwanted, or unlovable from time to time. We can't exist in a perpetual state of perfect confidence. But that doesn't detract from your queenliness. In fact, a queen can still be magical, can still emit divine essence and beauty, when she herself doesn't feel that way on the inside. Bad days are normal.

Here is a simple recipe for self-love, a little pick-me-up-magic, which you can do almost anytime and anywhere.

Materials

Cleansing herbs, such as palo santo

Rose quartz

Your favorite mug

Lavender tea (or flavor of your choice)

First, purify the rose quartz by burning an herb of your choice (like palo santo) and passing it over the crystal, washing it gently in cool water, or setting it beneath the moon or sun for some time. Place your clean, purified rose quartz into your favorite mug. Imbue it with the purpose of filling you with self-love. Ask it to send feelings of self-kindness and acceptance through you.

Next, pour your tea into the mug, raising energy to the things you love about yourself. (Lavender is an excellent herb for both love and purification—and it was historically used in Spain and Portugal as protection against evil).

Drink the tea silently, sip by sip, focusing on self-love. It can be difficult to quiet all the mental chatter, but continuously bring the mind back to your breath—and to the reasons you love yourself. You don't need to walk away feeling completely transformed, but you should walk away feeling like you took some time out for yourself. (For women who get their periods: This is a great time-out practice for bite-someone's-head-off PMS days.)

AN APOTHECARY OF MAGICAL HERBS, FLOWERS, AND PLANTS

The natural world is our greatest friend—if treated with respect. Did you know that aspirin comes from willow bark, and morphine from poppy seed?

Plants and herbs have been used for thousands of years all over the world—from the ancient Egyptians, who turned to hibiscus to help ease respiratory infections, to the indigenous Americans, who used wild rose to alleviate cold-like symptoms. Witches, of course, throughout myriad times and places, have also turned to nature for remedies, just as villagers and ordinary folk would do in times of need.

Communing and collaborating with nature can boost your magical craft. Just don't go using anything you don't know about, and be sure to check with your doctor first, as some of these natural goodies could potentially make you sick or contraindicate with other medicines.

Common medicinal herbs, flowers, and plants include:

Aloe vera: used to soothe irritated or sunburned skin

Echinacea: promotes healing from a cold or flu

Feverfew: used to reduce migraine pain

Ginger: settles the stomach

Ginseng: energy-inducing

Lavender: used to promote sleep and calm

Mugwort: promotes stomach, liver, and menstrual health

Peppermint: aids in digestion and cools the skin

St.-John's wort: stabilizes mood

Tea tree oil: used to cleanse the skin and ward off colds

Turmeric: anti-inflammatory, especially for arthritis

Valerian: promotes sleep

Violet: used to relieve irritated skin and calm the nerves

Witch hazel: used to clean minor cuts and tone the skin

A Daily Practice for Sending Love to Someone Who Needs It

It's not always easy to show your feelings (romantic, platonic, or otherwise), just like it's not always easy for some people to feel comfortable accepting others' feelings of love. This is especially true if the person you love is not near you, or is sick, stressed, or deceased.

I've often found myself thinking, "I have all these feelings and no way to really show them," and this practice is wonderfully cathartic. The practice requires a dedicated jar, like a mason jar, that you'll use to hold your love notes.

Materials

Paper

Pen

Lipstick (optional)

Jar

At the end of the day, settle down after your evening routine and pull out a piece of paper. Write a short love note to whomever you're sending love to. It could be someone who passed on, or even someone you're not very close to. It could even be a friend whom you're not particularly jiving with. Whoever it is, write the truth. Write it clearly, and with the depth of your love.

Fold the note, and seal it with a kiss. This is where your optional lipstick comes in. I sometimes use vibrant plum, a royal blue, or a deep red. (I pick a shade that feels right for the person.) Place it into your jar and say:

I send [name] all of my love.

A Drawing Practice for Accepting Love from Your Community, Friends, Peers, or Family

If you've dealt with feelings of worthlessness—even if you're aware that these feelings aren't warranted—then you know they are incredibly hard to reverse. Let's be honest: No spell, practice, or ritual can unwind years of emotional armor and self-doubt. It's a process, and it's a nuanced one, and often requires professional help. In this magical practice, though, you'll focus on growing a garden of self-love, one that you can watch bloom over time.

Materials

Paper

Colored pencils

Paint

Markers, crayons, or other medium

Wall space where you can hang your art, or a box (a shoebox will do)

Tape (optional)

Long-stemmed roses, flowers, or leaves

On days when you struggle with accepting love from people, you'll want to sit down and draw (or paint or doodle) a representation of their love. What words did they use? How did this make you feel? Your art doesn't have to be fancy. It just has to be honest. Be conscious of your feelings and be compassionate with yourself.

You can hang your art up on the wall or, if you prefer, you can put it away somewhere safe and sacred to you (like in a special box). If you choose to hang up your art, you can create a beautiful display by hanging (taping) your roses upside down by the stem. You can also tape leaves or petals to the wall. Or you can place flower petals or leaves into your box of art.

Continue growing your collection, over time. Bit by bit, you might find that you are blooming.

A Healing Love Ritual for Your Younger Self

Many of us carry wounds throughout our lives. Our memories are heavy, laden with haunting experiences. And our hearts feel, at times, as though they are a photograph—snapped and stuck forever in a certain moment. We move forward through life temporally, but we stay behind, still feeling remnants of old pain. Is this you? You're not alone.

While an empathic therapist can help you thoroughly work through any lasting trauma, this spell will allow you to both honor and move away from the wounds of yesterday.

Materials

Blue candle (blue is ideal for forgiveness and healing)

Picture of yourself from the past (at the age you'd like to focus on), or your name on a paper as a substitute

Two long pieces of ribbon or string

Scissors

Light your candle and look at the picture of yourself. Tie the two pieces of ribbon together. One represents now, and one represents yesterday.

Say:

I honor my body, this life, from past to present.

Take conscious, deep breaths, and meditate on those old wounds and what your younger self experienced. Was she resilient? Was she afraid? Did she hate her body? Was she abused?

Think about you now. What are you trying to work through? Why do you want to move on?

Cut the two pieces of ribbon, severing your need to stay bonded to the past.

Blow out the candle and say:

I honor my wounds, but I release myself from the burdens of yesterday.

A Spell to Turn Feelings of Hate into an Act of Self-Love

There's nothing more exhausting than being trapped inside your own feelings of hate. Even if you know that hating—or seriously disliking—someone is counterintuitive to your emotional health, it's a reality. No shame! You are only human, and it takes time and work to undo strong feelings toward others, especially when they've abused or mistreated you.

This spell won't make you suddenly love or forgive someone. That's more nuanced and personal. It will, however, prevent those feelings and energies from draining you and making you sick. It will enable you to transmute hate into self-love.

Materials

White candle (white is traditionally used for healing and destroying negativity)

Small piece of paper

A couple inches of black ribbon

Light your candle. Focus on the person (or people) you feel negatively toward. If you can, say out loud how they make you feel. Are they racist? Are they toxic? Do you find yourself staring at their Instagram with feelings of jealousy? Are you exhausted by how they make you feel about yourself? It's okay to get vulgar and emotional here. This is your space. Acknowledge your autonomy and willingness to work through this.

Write the person's (or people's) name(s) down on a piece of paper and roll it into a scroll. Tie the black ribbon around it and knot it three times.

Say:

I bind my negative feelings about you from affecting my emotional and physical well-being.

Throw the scroll into the trash or light it on fire in a safe place, like your bathroom sink.

A New Moon Ritual to Attract a Lover or Lovers

The best time for manifestation, especially when it comes to bringing shiny new things like love or pleasure into your life, is during a new moon.

It doesn't matter if you're into polyamory, monogamy, or finding a third person to add to your bedroom play—you set your intention here. But because consent and safety are essential, this spell isn't to be cast on a particular person. Love spell ethics can be tricky: Does that person want to love you? Is the person you desire already with someone? Would your crush even be right for you?

There's a lot to navigate, and witches take different stances here. In short, I'm not a fan of bending anyone's will, so I let the universe do its magic and I remain open to whatever would naturally come my way.

The use of the apple here denotes love in all sorts of ways. Witches have seen the inside of an apple (arranged as a pentagram) as a symbol of fertility, while lore suggests eating (or bobbing for) apples can bring future love.

Materials

Warm bath

Bath salts or essential oils

Red candle (red is generally used to represent love and desire)

Your favorite perfume or scented oil

One red apple

Knife

Sachet bag or plastic baggy

Slip of paper

Pen

Dash of cinnamon

On the night of the new moon, draw yourself a bath. Fill it with bath salts and essential oils. Light your candle, and get into the water. Cleanse every inch of your body, especially the parts you find extra attractive and the ones you feel not so comfortable with.

This isn't about being "clean" for someone— it's about reveling in yourself, being vulnerable, and imbuing your body with the love you want to attract. This is especially important if you face any identity or body-image issues, or if you have a chronic illness that affects your relationship with your body.

While you're in the water, meditate on the right person for you and the scenario you'd like to play out. When you're ready, get

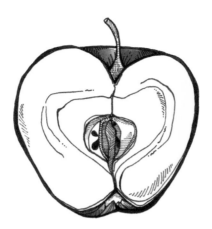

out of the tub. After you dry off, spray yourself with your favorite perfume or anoint yourself in scented oil. This scent will become a sort of magnetic force.

Go to your kitchen or any clean surface where you can slice your apple. Bring your candle with you. Carefully cut the apple in half and pluck all the seeds from the inside. Drop them into a sachet bag and spray that bag with your perfume or oil.

Close the sachet and say:

I am the earth and seed. I am the beloved and I am the lover.
As I move, I bloom. I bloom of love.

Next, write a letter to your future lover. It might say, "You are loyal and dependable," or "You are not possessive or controlling." You might even say, "You have great facial hair." Do it up! Sleep with the letter under your pillow for one night and then tuck it away in a drawer.

If you wish, sprinkle the apple with cinnamon and eat it slowly— taking in all the delicious mythology of the apple. Remember to carry the sachet bag with you so your lovers can find you. For an extra magical boost, wear your perfume on nights out or when you want to be found.

An Altar-Building Practice for Raising Your Love Vibes

Romantic love is not the only kind of love—it's reductive to say it is, especially given that everyone has a different way of experiencing love and desire. Love is about connecting your life to a bigger purpose, experiencing being alive and being inspired, showing gratitude and kindness, and constructing a world for yourself in which positive things happen. Obviously, this isn't la-la land and that's not always possible—but taking some time to raise those love vibes can help in larger ways that might not become apparent to you until you've spent some time cultivating them. You may already be doing some of these things—but now's the time to set intentions to it.

In this practice, you'll be reaping love's finest gifts by collecting, taking note of, engaging with, and sharing them.

Materials

Items that represent love to you

An area to use as an altar—a place to display a few items (a dresser top or shelf will do)

A camera or phone camera (optional)

Collect the items that represent love to you (e.g., a letter from a friend, a photograph, a gift, a family heirloom).

Display these items on your altar space; take time to arrange them, pausing on each item and reflecting on why it means something to you.

Continue adding to your altar whenever you feel you need to. Each day, stop by and look at it—remind yourself of your lovability and how much love is in your life.

Vow to show that same love to someone else as often as you can.

Snap photos of things that bring you happiness and share them on social media, if that feels right. Challenge yourself to share statuses of love weekly—to spread the love around and inspire others.

A Flower Magic Spell for Deepening the Ability to Love

If love were easy, we'd all give and receive it—no problem. Instead, it's wrapped up in all the things that make us who we are. It's messy and sad and hard and reluctant and full of poison and ache. It's human.

This spell will help you deepen your ability to feel it; it won't perfect your love or turn it into a cinematic cliché. It'll just remind you, through its physicality, that love requires focus—on the self and the other. No matter what kind of love. With this spell, you'll be creating a paste with crushed roses with which to write your love on paper.

Materials

Fresh petals (I prefer natural, undyed roses)

Mortar and pestle

A few drops of essential oil, coconut oil, or olive oil

A clean piece of paper

Ground yourself and focus on feeling and accepting love. Imagine any obstacles to that floating away, disintegrating in the air around you.

Take several petals and press them into the mortar. Use the pestle to crush them into a fine dust. This elbow grease is representative of the intention and energy put forth into cultivating a life of love.

Now, the fun part: Add some oil to this to create a paste. Make sure it's thick, goopy, and liquid enough to write with. (Save any extra for a face mask.)

Use the rose petal paste to write, with your fingertips, a message on a piece of blank paper. You can write messages like:

I am full of love.
I receive love.
I am alight in love.

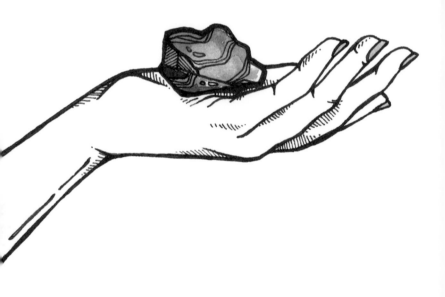

GRIEF AND TRAUMA

Finding Resilience and
Direction in Suffering

Life is, at best, a series of unpredictable happenings. They have the potential to elicit everything from pure joy to untold misery. Whether we've lost our lover after years of marriage, or we've lost ourselves after a traumatic event like an assault or illness, defending against that bleak sea of darkness can be difficult as its waves crash up onshore, threatening to pull us under.

The one thing we *can* do is choose how we respond. Do we wade into it, or do we sink? Sometimes traversing through rough waters is how we get past it. We have to take stock, recalibrate, and decide to heal. When I recently experienced three deaths in a short time, a friend told me that the only way to avoid suffering is by being in pain. Sit with that—it makes sense.

The rituals and practices in this chapter encourage you to feel as much as they encourage you to heal. Taking the time to tap into our grief and trauma means we won't expend so much energy repressing it. Much of our time is spent performing "okay-ness" to ourselves and others. We find ourselves nodding, smiling, and saying, "I'm great. How are you?" on autopilot, while inside we're breaking into shards. Grief has almost no language except silence, which is itself something to grieve. My hope is that you will give yours language. There is magic in wading through it.

As you move through this section, take care to check in with yourself:

- What traumas present themselves in your everyday life?
- What traumas are lingering deeper under the surface?
- What hurts?
- What sort of lessons have you learned while navigating the trauma and grief?
- Do you have any idea of what is causing the pain?
- Are there ways you can help others who are in pain?
- What sort of self-care can you perform to feel stronger?

A Bathing Ritual for Moving through Feelings of Grief

Death, loss, or other traumas may require a long healing process. Pain is a storm we move through, eventually leading us to the light.

After loss, you may find it hard to confront your sadness, denial, and anger. So much of grief is exercising "strength" or stoicism in public. It's exhausting. (I live in New York City, one of the best places for public crying.) This spell will help you transform sadness into strength. It takes place in a bathroom, with the door shut.

Materials

Photograph of your loved one, item that belonged to your loved one, or loved one's name written on paper

White candle

Bathtub

Essential oils (rose oil is potent and balanced)

Small piece of black obsidian (optional)

Set the photo, item, or paper on a counter where it won't get wet. Light the candle beside it. This mini altar represents your openness to confronting grief.

Draw yourself a bath (water is the element that allows us to submerge and move fluidly through our feelings). Prepare the space for introspection and safety. Fill the water with essential oils. Place your black obsidian, a dark stone that absorbs pain, on the rim of the tub. Step into the water and embrace your vulnerability. Take a few deep breaths and settle into silence.

Think of your grief as an organ: It holds suffering so it doesn't poison the rest of your body. But you must manage (and connect with) this organ to keep it functioning and receptive. Honor it, open it, let it fill you, and be filled by it. Feel free to cry, yell, or splash around.

If you want to, speak to the dead. Do what feels best for your grief: Nurture it, envision it surrounded by loving light, fill it with memories of your lost loved ones. Hold the obsidian and let it absorb your feelings.

When you are ready, rinse off, let the tub drain, and blow out the candle. Place the obsidian in moonlight or wash it in cool water to cleanse it.

A Spell to Banish
Recurring Nightmares

One of the ways trauma—and post-traumatic stress disorder in particular—affects people is through sleep disruption. It can be hard enough to fall asleep with racing, ruminating thoughts; then sometimes, when sleep finally comes, nightmares creep in and destroy it. Slumber is a precious healing tool for people in pain, and must be protected. This spell will help you take control of your sleep state, with the goal of banishing recurring nightmares. Please be sure to speak with a therapist if you continue to experience traumatic nightmares, though. You deserve care.

Materials

A pen

A piece of paper

A fireproof bowl

A sink

Matches

A charm—something small that symbolizes joy, such as a piece of rose quartz or a shell

First, write your recurring nightmare down on a piece of paper. If you can't write down all the details, don't. Use language that feels comfortable to you. After you've finished, say in a commanding manner:

I bind you, dark dreams, from casting shadows over me. My sleep is precious and lit by freedom. I am full of peace.

Repeat this until you feel powerful.

Set the fireproof bowl in the sink, and put the piece of paper into the bowl. Light the paper with your matches. Watch the paper burn, and then throw the ashes away.

Take your charm—whatever it is you feel symbolizes happiness and strength—and hold it in your hands. Imbue it with glistening, serene memories. This is your new sleep tool, and it's there to protect you. Sleep with it underneath your pillow.

A Ritual for Releasing
Parental Resentment

Like the poet Philip Larkin said, "They fuck you up, your mum and dad," and he wasn't wrong. Sometimes our parents actively hurt us with words and actions; other times their negligence is in the form of keeping us in a bubble or spoiling us. Sometimes our parents just feel like negative space.

Whatever the cause, resentment blooms over a lifetime, changing who we become and how we inhabit our lives. If resentment affects you, this spell will help you release it. As always, a trusted therapist should be your first port of call. You can do this spell if your parents are living or have passed on, because this is about releasing feelings—not necessarily letting your parents know. If possible, perform this during the full moon, a good time for releasing the old and deciding on the new.

Materials

A pen

A piece of paper

An envelope

A large bowl of water to submerge the envelope in

Begin by grounding. Clear your mind, then think how resentment has taken hold of your life. What do you resent? How did your parents hurt you? Were they conscious of it? Can you understand their behavior or motivations? How can compassion enter in?

Write it all down on paper, from the beginning to the present day. Include tangible examples of what affected you. Include any compassionate statements. If you are angry, be angry. If you're sad, be sad. If you're diplomatic, be diplomatic. Your feelings may morph over time, and this spell can serve as one step in an ever-evolving direction.

When you're done writing, put the paper in the envelope. Submerge the envelope in water. Make sure it is fully covered—watch the ink bleed through the paper. Leave the envelope soaking overnight and discard it the next day.

An Artistic Practice for Saying Good-Bye to Something You've Lost

Loss, either from death or because a friendship or relationship has gone up in smoke, is inevitable. Yet when you experience it, it feels wholly unique and earth-shattering, as if no one around you has ever felt it before, as if you are utterly alone and without direction. Sometimes the hardest thing to do is say good-bye. This spell can help you get comfortable with saying good-bye while helping you create something beautiful in the process.

Materials

One or two cups of tea—use rosemary tea, if you have it

A large piece of paper

Paint, markers, or colored pencils

A black ribbon

Set aside some time when you know you'll be alone. Drink your cup of tea (rosemary is excellent for banishing and disconnecting) while you move through this practice. Because it can be difficult to face these feelings, you'll only go for as long as your cup of tea lasts. (If you feel up for it, make two cups of tea.) While creating your art, don't worry about making a masterpiece. Be as melodramatic and honest as you need.

On your piece of paper, use your paint, markers, or colored pencils to draw or paint everything—memories, the name of the person you want to say good-bye to, phrases, shapes or objects that represent your former relationship. You can draw the person's face, their house, whatever represents them to you. The goal here is to train your mind to create beauty from loss, to transmute those feelings into something new and powerful. To show yourself that you can.

When you've finished your tea, stop working. Roll your piece into a scroll (if you're using paint, wait until it's dry, of course). Close it with your ribbon. Hide it away.

A Graveyard Meditation for Getting Comfortable with the Idea of Death

The Death-Positive Movement, started by Caitlin Doughty, who runs the Order of the Good Death, aims to get people comfortable with death by talking about it openly—instead of treating it like a taboo. Perhaps you've always felt uncomfortable with grief or maybe you've never been able to set foot in a funeral home. That is normal. It's painful, and we're socialized to avoid it.

Yet there is comfort in the natural cycle of time, life, and death. Witches honor this cycle by celebrating the changing seasons and the phases of the moon, and even purposefully being near death.

Materials

None

For this practice, unlike many of the others in this book, you're going to spend some time in a local graveyard. When you arrive, walk through it, breathing in and out and staying aware of your body: your breath, your feet touching the ground, the smells, the sights. Focus on your breath as you move—this is called a walking meditation.

Quieting the mind by focusing on your breath helps you hone your energy and intention. Yes, thoughts will crop up every few seconds, but you will go right back to concentrating on your breath.

As you move through the cemetery, stop at a tombstone that stands out to you (it could even be the tombstone of someone you love) or take a break on a bench and acknowledge that death is normal and natural, and that it happens to us all. Breathe through it, remaining conscious of how your living body is mixing and melding with the tombstones, the earth, and the dead. Thank the dead for allowing you to visit, and for showing you that the cycle of life is beautiful.

A Writing Practice for Confronting Complex Feelings of Grief

No grieving process is simple, but some losses are messy. I lost someone just before writing this book, and I was filled with confusion. I loved the person, but I didn't like him. And this weighed on me—until I learned that plenty of people feel this way and that it's very normal.

Maybe you've felt guilty for feeling some relief after someone passed. Maybe you have some regrets. Maybe you wished you did something or said something before the person left. Maybe you're angry at someone for dying. This poetry practice will help you sort through those feelings. It might not be the right exercise to do in the immediate days after a death, but it could be a good way to move through grief down the line.

Poets have always turned to the page to explore and capture the mystery and pain of death. One poet, e.e. cummings, wrote in his poem "Finis," "May I behold my sunset/Flooding/over silent waters."

Materials

Pen or pencil

Paper

Envelope (optional)

What does your grief look like to you? In this exercise, write a poem about your grief. Poetry is naturally very spacious and forgiving, since it lets you say something without necessary spelling it out literally.

Simply write as you see fit—write a poem to the person or about the person you're grieving.

Do with the poem afterward what feels right to you. You can keep it tucked away in an envelope, or you can throw it away.

A Ritual to Encourage Growth After a Traumatic Event

When I was in high school, I was put into foster care in a new school, in a new town, with a new family. That experience was scary, but it taught me inner strength. Still, I often felt very alone, like I was the black sheep in a sea of "normal." Looking back, I now know that this feeling of isolation taught me to find autonomy and happiness in small ways, through rituals and practices like this one.

I was so traumatized by being put into foster care that it took years for me to be able to speak or think about it. One way I did that was to reframe how I let the situation affect me. I'm sure you've had a dark time, too. But no matter what your experiences may have been like, giving yourself the time to grow is so important. This ritual will help you tap into—and grow—your strength and self-love.

Materials

A piece of paper

A pen

A jar

A flower or flower petals

Witch hazel

On a piece of paper, write down a difficult memory or incident and how it emotionally affected you. You can write as much or as little as you'd like.

Fold the paper and put it into the jar. Fill the jar with flower petals and witch hazel. The petals symbolize your ability to bloom despite your trauma, and the witch hazel removes negative energy and drowns out the trauma.

Take the jar outside to a garden and bury it deep in the soil. (City dwellers: You can also throw it in the garbage.) As you do, say:

My light cannot be eclipsed; from darkness I only rise. I rise and rise, in light, alight.

A Practice to Charge an Amulet for Psychic Protection from Abuse

These days, it can feel like we're surrounded by abusive behaviors and words—and that can be traumatic. Women and femme-presenting people receive an onslaught of negative messaging—from catcallers on the street to politicians in the news—not to mention the abuse many women face in their personal lives.

For this practice, you will charge an amulet with protective energy. Carry it on you.

Materials

An amulet of your choice—this could be a coin, small stone, crystal, button, or piece of jewelry

Cleanse the space in which you'll be working. A quick tidy will do—you don't want chaotic or messy energy while you focus and charge your amulet.

Set the object you chose before you and sit comfortably. Hold your palms out and visualize the energy of the universe radiating around you. Slowly bring your palms to face each other and rub them together until they're warm and you feel powerful. Hold them a few centimeters apart and build your energy, imbuing it with protection and love. Use this energy to charge your amulet.

When it feels like you've reached the epicenter of your charge, bring your hands over the object and infuse it. Don't stop until you feel the amulet is fully charged. This can be exhausting, since so much energy is being used. (You might do this before bed so that you can go right to sleep afterward.)

Once you've charmed your amulet, reach for it whenever you need it—move it between your palms or hold it to your chest. If it's a piece of jewelry, all you need to do is touch it to feel its magical, protective powers.

A Ritual for Comfort After the Loss of a Pet

The loss of a pet is such a difficult grief. Pets are your family, confidants, and support, always there to listen and experience life alongside you. And you've been there for your pet, watched their wild little quirks and kooky habits, comforted them when they've been sick or scared. Maybe you even found comfort in their late-night antics or full-moon energy bursts.

The pain can be multilayered: Loss is difficult to adapt to. Not seeing your little furball anymore can be traumatizing, especially if you're averse to change. Knowing that they may have suffered, or that you might have had to make the hard choice to end it, is heartbreaking. This ritual can help you acknowledge your loss while honoring your pet's happy moments. Do this when you have time to mourn and burn a candle, so preferably a few hours.

Materials

A black candle

Pictures of your pet

Their toys, or anything that you feel represented their happiest moments

A pen

A piece of paper

An envelope

Light the candle—preferably in a spot your pet loved. Next to the candle, place their picture and toys. Think about or talk to your pet—what will you say? If it feels right, you can sit silently. When you feel ready, write a letter to your pet. Don't worry: It doesn't have to be your last communication, just what you want to say right now. If you have the time, let the candle burn itself out. Keep the letter in an envelope until you feel ready to either dispose of it or put it away for good.

NEGATIVITY

———

Lighting the Way When Everything Goes Dark

Do you ever feel like the world—even the moon and the sun!—is your enemy? And let's not get started on Mercury retrograde.

Sometimes you're trying so hard to just function, but the seams are splitting. You can feel the light around you dimming, becoming foggy, murky, polluted.

The spells, rituals, and practices in this chapter are designed for those moments when your world weariness has nearly taken over—when protesting and resisting and commuting and trying and hurting have gotten into the core of your bones. These practices are designed to give you back your autonomy and enchantment, so that you can think, feel, decompress, and forgive. So that you can shimmer again.

As you move through the spells in this chapter, remember that the most powerful thing you can do is keep a careful record of your emotional and psychic well-being. Start by using your journal to record your feelings: Are you resentful? Angry? Do you feel like you wake up in a bad mood? After you've worked a spell or ritual, do you feel lighter? Less angry? More intuitive? Take note of these changes—and what you think may have contributed to the change.

Many magic practitioners believe that what you bring to the table is what you get. If you sew crops of negativity, you will reap it for the year to come. Put into your practice what you want to take from it: positivity, respect, honor.

That said, the one thing this book is not is chronically positive. That's because darkness and light, and all of those various, married energies—both the negative and the positive ones—coexist; that duality (and the gray in-between) is what makes our lives meaningful.

Positivity is useful, but it's often linked with privilege. We all have light and dark times. With magic, all humans are on equal footing. Magic asks us to work through our emotions (all of them) and direct our intent—not to pretend we don't feel badly. If you can bring a genuine desire to overcome, to grow, to find a way to transform your negativity through magic, that's the goal.

A Ritual to Get Rid of Imposter Syndrome

You walk into a meeting surrounded by your talented, fabulous peers, who are telling you exactly how talented and fabulous you are. But you have the sense that you're hiding a wild secret: You're not actually talented, you're not fabulous, and you don't even know why you're there.

Your accomplishments feel like a misrepresentation of who you "really" are—a failure—and soon enough, everyone will find out. You don't deserve success. You didn't work hard enough. Your voice doesn't matter.

This is imposter syndrome, and even witches aren't immune to it. This spell will help you overcome and rewire that complex web of feelings.

Materials

A small handheld mirror

A small gift for yourself—a cup of coffee, a new crystal, a single rose, a new deck of cards, a tube of lipstick, a pair of socks, whatever you like

A pen

A piece of paper

Gaze into the mirror. See your eyes, your skin, your hair. Now see beyond your exterior. Shut your eyes and think about your accomplishments, even if the imposter voice chimes in. Pool them in your mind, making a mental slideshow. Every time you think of an accomplishment, big or small, say:

I made this happen.

Give yourself your gift. Thank yourself for your accomplishments and acknowledge that you made them happen. List them on paper. Number them so each is unique and separate. Carry this magical reminder with you, so you can reread it whenever you need to. Reach for it when you feel the imposter creep in. Reroute your mental energy by switching to positive thoughts when a negative one pops up; it takes practice and intent, but with that extra dose of magic, you'll start a new habit.

An Earthing Activity to Reduce Stress from Political Chaos

Do you ever wake up and feel like you're living in a different reality? If you're anything like me, you may expend a great deal of your personal emotional energy and labor during times of intense political turmoil—and it's exhausting, especially if you're without inspiring leaders or supportive communities.

If you've lost hours to the news, labored over racist or sexist comments on social media, or dealt with family members whose political ideologies feel like an attack on your person (you're not alone), you know how hard it is to catch a break. I find it nearly impossible to respond to the hateful things I read the second I wake up, but I do try to give myself some time to mindfully disengage.

To resist, create revolution, break stigmas, and educate others, we need all our energy and vision—but we can't exactly resist or advocate for our beliefs when our bodies and minds aren't well nurtured.

This is a sort of ritualized practice I do when the tides get rough, when I start feeling myself go numb, and when I lose sight of the fact that this world still does offer empathic and compassionate energies Best part: It's doable pretty much anywhere.

Materials

A backyard, local park, or garden

A bag

Head to a local park or a community garden and simply take fifteen minutes to breathe deeply—in through your nose, out through your mouth—as you gaze at the raw nature that surrounds you.

Notice everything. What colors do you see? What do you smell? Is there water? Is the soil wet? Are there leaves falling? Are there insects buzzing? Remind yourself that we are all made of the same star stuff that created this earth and its elements.

Next, collect some fallen leaves or flower petals, or stones, and gather them in your bag. (It's always nice to ask the earth first.) Run your hand through blades of grass, and take off your shoes to feel the earth under your feet. Whatever your beliefs, nature has an innate magic. In fact, according to many studies, spending time in nature can lower your blood pressure, reduce your heart rate, and limit the production of stress hormones.

Bring your collection home. Scrapbook the leaves or petals, or set the stones upon your bedside table. Let these items symbolize rest and regeneration, and turn to them when you need a moment after a long day. Let them serve as a reminder to consciously disconnect when you need to.

You can make this a weekly ritual for decompressing after dealing with triggering world affairs.

EARTHING: MOTHER NATURE'S MOOD MAGIC

The Journal of Inflammation Research found that earthing—connecting with nature by direct skin contact with the surface or waters of the earth—can have profound effects on our health and happiness. That's because touching the earth is electrically conductive.

A 2015 a study published by the *Proceedings of the National Academy of Sciences* in the United States found that being in nature calms the part of your brain that is responsible for depression and worry. By taking a walk in the woods or jogging along the beach, you can ease muscular tension, reduce blood pressure, decrease your heart rate, and reduce stress hormones.

Visit a small garden, the beach, or a public park regularly. This can feed your inner magic by helping you ground and focus.

Nature Practices for Negativity Busting

Witches and nature go hand in hand. We may not all work with or in nature, but having a relationship to the elements—and the cosmos—is central for many practitioners. Filling your home with flowers, plants, herbs, and crystals can help you connect with nature in simple and meaningful ways. These practices can help you oust negativity from your daily life.

Materials

Peace lily

Sage

Essential oil (lavender or rosemary)

Holy basil/tulsi

Spending some time with nature, as we explore in Earthing: Mother Nature's Mood Magic (page 61), is a wonderful way of relieving stress and connecting to the power of the world around you. It is affordable and easy, and it can help you grow your green thumb.

Try decorating your home in the following ways:

Buy a peace lily. Peace lilies are excellent additions to your home. They're said to detox the air and symbolize love, harmony, and peace.

Grow sage in your home. Sage is a favorite herb among witches—not only is it used in smoke cleansing but it's also known to promote wisdom and strength. It can be used to make tea and hair rinses, and to promote digestion. I recommend reading the *Old Farmer's Almanac* for detailed instructions on how to grow it. (You can also find this information easily on the Internet.)

Start by planting sage seeds or using cuttings from a grown sage plant. This isn't a quick process. Devote time and energy to cultivating such a magical and resilient plant; it can help you let the worries of the day fall away into nature's generosity.

Wear or bathe in lavender or rosemary essential oil. If keeping plants in your home is a no-go, you can add nature to your space by infusing it in your everyday lifestyle. Lavender is associated with happiness and peace, while rosemary is used in cleansing and blessing. You can tap into these herbs' powers by dabbing an essential oil on your wrists, dropping the oil into a bath, or adding a bit of oil to a spray bottle.

Keep holy basil in your home. Holy basil—also known as tulsi—is a plant originally from India that is used in Ayurvedic medicine. It's an adaptogen, which is a natural compound that can help you conquer stress and remain positive in the face of chaos or crisis. Its long list of medicinal uses includes relieving the flu, asthma, upset stomach, and more. It's said to provide a spiritual boost, attracting happy vibrations in any environment. You can find holy basil in tea form, which is both delicious and easy to brew.

Devote time and energy to cultivating a magical and resilient plant.

A Practice to Shield Yourself from External Negative Energies

Everywhere we go, we're around all sorts of energies. Sometimes, they're chaotic, frenetic, angry, intense, or sad, and they can seep into our personal space and poisonous. Whether we're conscious of this or not, our minds naturally want to deflect that energy—which ends up depleting a lot of our own.

This practice will help you armor up—whether you're dodging energy bullets in a crowded place or simply dealing with a friend in a nasty mood.

Materials

None

Stop somewhere you can plant your feet. Take a few deep breaths—in through your nose, out through your mouth—and then say aloud or silently think to yourself:

Whether you mean well or not, and whether you intend to or not, you cannot have my energy, light, or joy. I am protected.

Next, envision a shield of white, shimmering light surrounding your body. It should start small—at first just outlining your body. Depending on how you feel, you may want to expand it, making it wider so that it reaches as far as five feet around you. (This is especially helpful when in crowded areas like a busy bus station or shopping mall.)

As the shield surrounds you, imagine a small hole at the very bottom, right at your feet. Imagine any negative energy seeping out. You may envision this as gray or static. See it leaving, being replaced only by shimmering white light. Plug the hole and bask in this beautiful, protective energy, knowing that whatever comes your way will bounce right off you.

A Besom-Building Practice for Cleansing a Space of Negativity

To protect or rid a house of negativity, a sweeping-away with a besom—a common tool in Wicca, a branch of Paganism—can do the trick. Magical brooms, besoms are usually made from wood and natural bristles.

A besom allows its user to actively and physically sweep any negative energies out the door. A homemade one can help you feel even more connected to your intentions.

There are plenty of ways to make a besom—and many materials to make it with. (Sometimes the materials used correlate to the magic being performed.)

Materials

A sturdy staff (or handle) of oak, ash, or other local wood (about 3 to 4 feet [0.9 to 1.2 m] tall)

Several thin but strong branches, each about 1 foot (30 cm) long (mugwort or thyme are common, but any thin sticks will do)

1 or 2 dried lavender bundles (optional)

A strong cord or rope

Lay your sturdy staff on the ground. Carefully place your branches alongside it, up against the staff at one end. Add the dried lavender bundles alongside the branches, if you're using them. (Lavender is commonly used to customize a besom, making it extra pretty and leaving a sweet lavender scent as you magically cleanse your space.)

Wrap the cord tightly around the branches and lavender to tie them to the staff. You may smoke-cleanse or simply meditate on the besom, connecting to it, and envisioning it clear and ready to use. You can use your broom to "shoo" away the negativity. This besom may not be strong enough to use for real cleaning (and it could damage your floor), but you can mime the act of sweeping. Be mindful as you perform your sweeping, and use it when you feel your home or a room needs to be cleared of negative energy.

A Serenity Ritual for Powerlessness

Growing up, my mother always said the serenity prayer:

> *God, grant me the serenity to accept the things I cannot change; courage to change the things I can; and wisdom to know the difference.*

Although neither of us is religious, it always comforted me, especially in times when I felt like life was spiraling out of control. In this ritual, I borrow from that prayer and adapt it to a magical practice.

Materials

A small item that represents you (e.g., a piece of jewelry or a photograph of yourself)

5 stones from outside or 5 crystals of your choice (smoky quartz works well for clarity of mind and cleansing); they should be cleansed with water or smoke

Sit at a clean, neat space—perhaps at your altar or at a desk near a window. Place the item that represents you in front of you. Focus on what is troubling you and causing you to lose a sense of control or balance. Focus on what you can change. Focus on what you cannot change.

Slowly, place each stone around the photograph or item. This act grounds you to the earth, reminding you that time will reveal all—whether in your favor or not. Say:

I am serene
in knowing what I can create,
what I cannot,
and where the shadow falls between.

Leave the stones out for as long as you need to, contemplating your serenity and the wisdom that comes with acceptance.

A Practice for Honoring Your Truth After Experiencing Gaslighting

Gaslighting is when someone—perhaps a spouse, a friend, your doctor, or your boss—makes you question your reality. It's a form of manipulation that makes you doubt yourself. Many times, people don't even realize they've been gaslighted, even though they may have a sense that an interaction was problematic and toxic.

If you've been gaslighted, it's important that you do what you can to stay safe and find support. This practice can help you find comfort and honor your own voice in the aftermath. Many spells help us block energies, but magic can't stop an asshole from being an asshole. So, this simple practice reroutes your focus back onto you, by letting you speak your truth.

Materials

A small doll or figure (you can even draw it) that will act as a listener

A self-care treat (such as taking a bath, doing a face mask, eating a cookie, or watching a film you love)

Simply talk to your listener. Tell it everything you experienced; tell it your truth. Say your truth loudly, and say every detail. Repeat ideas or sentences if you must. Pay special attention to anything you were made to doubt or question. Know that this figure is listening.

Once your listener has your truth, it's self-care time. Treat yourself. Need some more ideas? Do something fun, wild, sexy. Dance in your underwear, blast music, eat cake, binge-watch a show, read a book of poetry, take a bubble bath.

A Morning Tarot Ritual to Make Your Commute More Productive

Do you ever feel claustrophobic or physically (or psychically) tired from squeezing into a tube or a bumpy bus every day? You're not alone. This ritual can help you start your commute off right, and it can be modified for people who work from home, drive, bike, walk, or take any other mode of transportation.

Materials

Tarot deck

Corresponding guide to the cards (or the Internet)

If you're walking, driving, or biking to work, do this before you leave. If you take public transportation, you can do it while commuting. And if you work from home, do it before kicking off your to-do list.

Shuffle and hold your tarot deck in one hand. Clear your mind, take a few deep breaths, and ask a question for the day. It might be, "How can I be my best self today?" or "How can I ensure confidence at work?" Pull a single card from the deck—one that calls out to you.

Tarot cards offer ideas and symbols to think about in context to your life. You can read your tarot deck's guide to the cards or even check the Internet for interpretations. Gaze at the image on the card. Does it speak to you?

You might draw the Hanged Man, which indicates suspension or being caught in limbo but can also signify walking away. Or, you might pull the World—which could lead you to celebrate your queenliness after a work triumph—or the Two of Wands, which asks you to push for progress or planning.

During your commute, meditate on the card's lesson and how it might affect your day or your future. Concentrating on an idea or lesson can ground you in your day and help you focus or manifest. Place your pulled card next to your workspace for the day as a gentle reminder.

TAROT

Tarot cards have been used for divination (the act of gaining insight) since the eighteenth century. There is some debate over the origin of tarot cards, but generally, they're thought to have appeared first in the fifteenth century as playing cards—brought to Europe from Egypt. Modern decks typically contain four suits—swords, cups, coins (also called pentacles), and wands (or batons). They're also made up of the Major Arcana (symbols or archetypes, like Death or Justice) and the Minor Arcana (four of coins, six of wands, etc.). There are variations across decks according to an artists' vision, and even the meanings of certain cards can change according to the creator.

The tarot showcases, by way of its imagery, a spectrum of human emotion and circumstance. While many believe the tarot yields answers served up by the divine, or by the universe's wise energies, others believe the drawing of a card is random—allowing us, no matter our belief or practice, to meditate on what we've pulled.

You can use the tarot by pulling a single card each day. Prop up the card on your altar, dresser, or even the dashboard of your car. By doing this, you can create a ritual to:

- Simply meditate on the card's imagery and meaning
- Draw, paint, or write based on its meaning
- Let it inspire your daily look
- Find a new way to think about your situation or circumstance
- Use it as your guiding light for the day

A Gratitude Journaling Practice to Lighten a Bad Mood

My mother gave me a journal as a gift once. She said, "You can only use this for beautiful, light things—like your best memories and what you're grateful for." It caught me off-guard; we often journal through our pain and trauma but not the things that make our lives beautiful. In this practice, you'll not only journal about what you're grateful for, but you'll also actively identify ways to reap more of the good stuff in your life.

Materials

A dedicated gratitude notebook

Something to write with

At the end of your day, open to a page in your notebook and draw a line down the center of it. On one side write, "I'm grateful for" and on the other write, "I manifest."

In the "I'm grateful for" column, list three to five things that you are grateful for that day. It can range from "My barista was kind to me" to "My ability to pay for my medication" to "The weather." Don't worry if these are the same every day. That's a good thing!

In the other column, write down ways that you could keep the gratitude—and what causes it—flowing. It could be that you manifest "A good work ethic" or "Kindness" or "An ability to appreciate what I have."

By reminding yourself of these things daily, you're able to create more of them in your day-to-day life. A big part of magic is believing that something already exists—even without candles, an incantation, or any other tools. In this case, the magic is in your written word.

SIMPLE MAGICAL PRACTICES TO BANISH NEGATIVITY AND MAKE ROOM FOR THE LIGHT

Get rose quartz. This crystal is great to keep on your person and to have in your bedroom or any area of the house where you go to decompress after a long day. Rose quartz is known to radiate feelings of love and compassion. You can even sleep with this crystal under your pillow.

Give someone a compliment. Your word is magic, so say something kind. It will instantly boost someone's day while making you feel good. Kindness is contagious.

Make a besom. A besom is a witch's broom, usually made out of wood and natural bristles. One German custom says that to keep negativity out of the house or to rid negativity that came into it, a sweeping-away with a witch's besom could do the trick. You can make your own besom with bits of wood and any sort of natural bristle, like thin birch branches, straw, or twigs, or you can designate a special, ordinary broom to do the work. See page 65 for more on besoms.

Burn cedar. Cedar has been used by many cultures to clear an area of energies and restore it. It's healing, calming, and peace-promoting—and it can be found almost anywhere, from occult shops to websites to even your local clothing boutique.

REGENERATION
AND RECHARGE

Making Space for Renewal
and Self-Transformation

If chapter 3 was about kicking the negative, this chapter is about rebirth, taking that blank slate—freshly stripped of toxic residue—and giving it back its magical sheen.

The concept of regeneration or rebirth touches many myths and religious beliefs. But we aren't talking about growing new body parts or rising from the dead.

We're going to be casting spells and performing rituals and practices for everyday renewal—for ending a creative block, taking an astrological breather, or tapping into the symbolic fluidity of the mermaid. So, in short: Have fun with it! Use it to remind yourself of what makes you feel alive and electric, what makes sense to your life as a whole, what sort of fun activities you want to do more of.

It may sound exceedingly simple, but because we're so caught up in the minutiae of everyday life, we tend to lose sight of the magic in saying yes to what we want and no to what doesn't serve us. We also forget that we are energetic beings that also need to recharge, need downtime, need sleep, and need care.

You are natural, you are flora; you must be watered, you must see the sun. So while you are working through this chapter, be mindful of your body. Do you need to breathe, stretch, drink water? Be mindful of your energy levels. Do you need to send some color into your blood? Say yes to the little things that make you vibrate.

A Mermaid Ritual to Promote
Going with the Flow

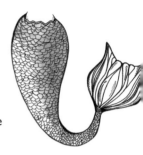

If you're the kind of person who always seeks a sense of control or if you simply have a hard time letting go—whether it's during projects at work or just making downtime for yourself at home—this mermaid ritual can help.

The mermaid, an enduring symbol, is the ocean's representative—mysterious and fluid, ruled by the changing tides. In this ritual, the ocean's powers and the archetype of the mermaid will help you let loose.

Materials

A warm bath

Your favorite essential oil or bath salts

Moonlight

Disconnect from all technology so you won't feel the need to respond to anyone. Draw a bath. Sprinkle in some essential oils, bath salts, or some table salt (saltwater is one way of making sea magic). Meditate on how the ocean changes, daily and hourly. Think about how those tides might inspire your life. Maybe you wouldn't be so stuck on one idea or one single path if you felt more comfortable adapting to high tide, low tide, or stormy seas.

There's a beautiful Sanskrit phrase, *"Om namo narayani,"* which translates to "I surrender to the divine." Sanskrit is a beautiful language, but if you'd prefer to paraphrase, you might say, "I trust the universe to do what is best for me."

Speak this to yourself as you sink into the warm, glorious water. Become a mermaid—thank the water for showing you how freeing it is to move fluidly, to change forms, to give in to the tide.

When you get out of the water, find the moon, if you can. Dry off in its light (outside or at a window) while thinking about how it controls the ocean. Remember that there are some elements that you cannot entirely control.

A New Moon Ritual for Kicking a Creative Block

If you've ever hit a wall creatively, you know the sting of a blank page staring back. Unwritten work, unfinished paintings. Your heart feels like a blank canvas begging for color, but it remains undone. Unfulfilled creative urges can weigh heavily, which is why this practice allows you to get those creative energies flowing.

Begin this ritual on the day of the new moon. It will last five days.

Materials

Tarot deck

Pen

Journal

White candle

At the end of each night, pull one tarot card. Look at its corresponding meaning and journal about how the selected card might associate with your work. You can focus on the imagery and write down ideas that inspire you, or you can focus on the card's story and how it meshes with your own as an artist. You can also journal about how the lesson in the card corresponds to your piece of art.

Be creative. Make lists of ideas; allow for stream of conscious. What do you feel? What do you think? Nothing is irrelevant. When you move through all the junk, you might find gold. As a creator, you must sow the seeds to reap the garden.

At the end of the fifth night, display your tarot cards: Make an altar or simply prop them up on your desk.

Light a white candle and say:

I am creative. I am generative. I am prolific. I have planted a garden of ideas and it blossoms bright.

MOON PHASE MAGIC

For millennia, people have harnessed the moon's undeniable powers. Our Luna is a powerful symbol of nature, time, and the cycles of life. She keeps us steady and stable, synced temporally and emotionally. Many witches cast spells according to the moon's given phase. For example, around the new moon, I often notice a sense of gentle drive and imagination—which makes it easy for me to calibrate my practices in ways that work with the moon. I might focus on that drive and creativity to conjure up a plan or set power to a goal. Keeping a moon journal can help you get into a rhythm with moon magic and your moods during the phases.

The new moon, a time for seedling dreams and goals, is *the* time for manifestation. It helps boost your spell work, and adds extra oomph to your wishes and intentions. During this time you can kick off a plan; start something you've been dreaming of doing; create a wish jar; visualize your goals; or cast a spell for opportunities.

The full moon is generally considered to be the most potent lunar phase, kicking your magic up a few notches. It's a great time for spells and rituals that require you to do the tough work—binding, banishing, removing barriers, and working on yourself in potent ways. Where the new moon is good for bringing or pulling in, the full moon is great for almost anything, especially kicking to the curb unwanted ideas, feelings, or toxic people's effects on you.

Since **the waning moon** is all about the vanishing moon, focus on using this moon to banish, remove, bind, or say good-bye.

The waxing moon provides opportunity to add a new ritual or routine to your life, focus on a new project, or cast a spell to bring something to fruition.

The daily moon. Each day, the moon also moves through the twelve astrological houses, so it's worth finding out what it means when the daily moon is in a certain house. To use the daily moon in your magical practice, see "An Inspirational Zodiac Practice for When You Need Some Celestial Mojo," page 80.

A Spell to End Loneliness and Conjure New Friendship

People rarely admit it, but making new friends is not always easy, especially during times of transition, like leaving college or moving to a new city, or even deciding to say good-bye to a group of toxic, not-so-great friends. In this spell, you will break down barriers to new friendships—leaving you open to beautiful, magical, mutually respectful new relationships.

Materials

White candle

Pen

A small piece of paper

An envelope

During the new moon—when manifestation practices are strongest—take a moment before bed to perform this spell. When you wake up, you'll start the day knowing that you've removed anything in the way of new friendship.

Light the candle and sit for a moment with your thoughts. Visualize what sort of friends you'd like to have. Are they supportive, creative, open-minded? Think about what you can offer your friends, too—maybe you're loyal, optimistic, and radically vulnerable—and the qualities you possess that you'd like others to appreciate.

On your piece of paper, write down this statement:

The new moon has brought a gift.
A friend, a light, a come-true dream,
a friendship as wild and as beautiful as the sky.

Say this statement aloud, as well.

Pour a bit of the wax onto the paper, fold it, and put it into the envelope. Carry the envelope with you throughout the day.

A Ritual to Celebrate Yourself After You've Lost Self-Confidence

If you've ever taken a major hit to your self-confidence—you got laid off, you did your assignment all wrong, you failed a test, you didn't land the job—then you know how hard it can be to get your mojo back. You feel like a wilted flower, passed over. This ritual will get you thinking about why you're absolutely magical, so you can start feeling like yourself again.

Materials

7 small candles, each in a different color to represent the different days of the week

A container, like an empty coffee can or a large sachet bag

Do this ritual over seven days. Select seven colored candles, one for each day of the ritual. The colors should correspond to an element of your personality that you love and want to celebrate. For example, a red candle might symbolize your fiery passion, while a light-blue candle might represent your ability to go with the flow, like water.

At either the end or the beginning of the day, light one candle. Envision how that color represents an element of who you are. Think about why that element is so powerful, so lovable. Envision your body emanating with that quality. Bask in it.

As you concentrate each day, say:

I am _____ and this is enough.

Fill in the blank with whatever word or phrase you've chosen for that day. It might be something like "trying" or "alive."

Burn each candle for as long as you can each day. At the end of each day, place your candle in your container. Sleep with it near your pillow. On the seventh day, charge your container under the moon's light. Then it will always be a symbol for why you're so amazing.

An Inspirational Zodiac Practice for When You Need Some Celestial Mojo

Whether you believe in astrology or not, you can use the qualities of each zodiac sign as tools to boost your spirits, dial up your happiness, and remove blocks.

Materials

None

For this practice, you'll want to find out which astrological house the moon is passing through on a given day. For example, the mood might be a little more Aries one day, or a little more Scorpio another.

From there, you'll want to ask these questions:

- What can I learn from the moon being in this sign today?
- How can this moon inspire me to be a better version of myself?
- How do I like the moon in this sign?
- Is today a good day to make plans and get stuff done?
- Should I spend some time doing self-care today?

When the moon is in the signs below, you'll want to . . .

 Aries: Think things out, drink a glass of wine, finalize projects, not rush to conclusions

 Taurus: Get to work on projects, enjoy life, take a nap, be mellow, tend to some gardening, meditate in nature

 Gemini: Communicate ideas, make things happen, finish your task list, be the life of the party, make a killer playlist for the week ahead

 Cancer: Allow yourself to feel things strongly, organize your closet, celebrate your vulnerabilities, take a bubble bath, help others

Leo: Be ridiculous, have a party, create things, show your feelings, start a workout regimen, make bold moves

 Virgo: Organize your things, take stock, find gratitude, prepare meals

 Libra: Make deals, make love, say you're sorry, go to a meetup, check in with your friends

 Scorpio: Focus intensely on your intentions, focus on positive energies rather than dwelling on the negative, avoid rabbit holes, have amazing sex, use glamour magic, meditate

 Sagittarius: Create a bucket list, complete something on your bucket list, remain grounded—but have fun

 Capricorn: Apply for a job, pamper yourself after a task well done, keep your head down and finish something

 Aquarius: Think outside the box, start an uprising, create something amazing, dress vividly, laugh out loud

 Pisces: Read a beautiful book, make floral arrangements, go to the beach, visualize dreams, dance in your undies to pop music

A Spell to Recharge After Attending a Protest or Doing Social Justice Work

Wanting more, wanting better, and wanting equality is good—and it's worth fighting for. In fact, many witches would say that resistance is part and parcel of an ethical craft. Using your privilege, be it your platform, your voice, or your vote, is a form of magic. However, social activism and protest can be emotionally and physically draining.

In this spell, you'll be able to recalibrate and focus on recharging your energies after acts of protest and resistance, or even simply engaging with trolls on the Internet.

Materials

A bowl of lukewarm water

Your favorite essential oil

To your bowl with lukewarm water, add a few drops of your favorite essential oil. (Lavender is great for tranquility, while rose is good for love.) Place one palm up, facing the sky, and place one palm over the water, facing down.

With the face-up palm, begin to envision the universe's energy coming into you. Feel it charging through you as a pure, white light. Say:

I ask for the energy to stay active, healthy, and efficient. I ask to be replenished. I am a tower of strength and power.

Imagine that energy moving through you toward your other palm. Pour that white light into the water. When you feel you've sufficiently charged the water, wash your hands in it, rubbing them carefully together, making it a point to care for your body. Enjoy this moment for yourself, and repeat whenever you need to recharge your energies lost to resistance work.

A Ritual to Conjure Sensuality When You're Not Feeling Very Sexy

When you're working, raising a family, dealing with a crazy commute, and handling health issues, or when you're simply out of steam, your sex life can take a hit. That's all right, *bebe*. You can still connect with your body and enjoy feeling the love.

For any time you feel like you want to get back in touch with the Scorpio in you (Scorps are ruled by Pluto, and all the super chthonic things, like death and sexuality), this pick-me-up ritual involving the archetypes of the Egyptian god Bes (god of music and sexual pleasure, and, awesomely, helping birth babies) and goddess Bastet (goddess of perfume and protection and, amazingly, cats) will get you moving and feeling divine.

Materials

Comfortable or sexy clothes (or none at all!)

Red candle

Perfume, cologne, or essential oil

Sexy music

Slip into something cozy or sexy, or wear nothing at all! Light your candle, spritz a bit of perfume/cologne or oil on your skin. State:

I ask Bes and Bastet to fill me with a sense of pleasure and desire. I celebrate and honor my body and its sacred sensuality.

Put on your music and dance. Go wild. Think about the way your body moves and feels as you dance. Think about how your scent sways in the air as you move. Notice how body and fragrance are linked—a perfume wears differently on everyone.

Don't ascribe to traditional ways of "sexy dancing"—just move. You don't have to be anyone, represent any gender, fulfill any social role— just be you in your glorious natural state.

When you're ready to end your ritual, snuff out the red candle. Take a moment to appreciate your own power.

A Spell for Lunar
Light Acceleration

When you're dealing with a lot and you just need to get to the end of the week, this speed-up spell is a good way to get your bearings and facilitate that process.

Sometimes you just need an answer. Maybe you're preparing your life for the next big step. This spell can be used in any of those capacities, as long as you enter into it with the knowledge that it doesn't change time or cause time travel, because, well, science.

It will, however, ground you in the present and instill in you the fortitude and patience to get through what you need to get through.

Materials

A time-telling device—an hourglass, a watch, even a drawing of a clock

A clear quartz

Sit in a place that is comfortable for you and near a window—or, even better, in the direct path of moonlight—and set your time-telling device before you. Ground yourself in the present, acknowledging that it is important to experience the here and now—even if you can't wait to hurry the hell up and get past the dark times. Hold your clear quartz in an open palm and under or in the pathway of the moon's light. Speak:

The moon moves time in my favor,
that it imbues me with a glimmering alive-ness,
that it carves my wildest dreams,
harming none in its path.

Concentrate on the moon's light charging your crystal. Mentally focus on programming it to become your friend, your guide, and a symbol of your patience, as the next few days or weeks go by. Keep it on you in your pocket (or purse or tote or on your desk) at all times and hold it when you need to be reminded that you are moving through the process and you will get to the other side.

A Moodboard Ritual for Making Things Happen

Need to rejuvenate your life in some way? You don't have to wait until New Year's Eve to make a resolution. Maybe you need to revamp your closet or work on developing a new, more confident you after scoring a big-deal job. Maybe you just need to stop using social media for a while.

In this moon-shattering ritual, you'll make a magical moodboard that will help you pull your ideas and inspirations together. It will help you meditate on your ideas and integrate them into your day-to-day life.

Materials

Magazines, books, tarot cards, or any visual images of your archetype; pen and paper work too

Paper and glue, or a photo album

Yellow candle

Look through magazines, books, and other media. Find images that represent your goal or your ideal self. If you can't find the right images, you can also draw them. If you're looking to amp up your confidence, you might cut out pictures of people who deliver serious fierceness. You might print out an image of a tarot card that represents an archetype that inspires you.

Once you've collected these images, put them together as a moodboard. You can paste them onto a piece of paper or arrange them in a photo album that can be your own magical flipbook.

Add to your moodboard as often as you want, and dazzle it up with glitter, flower petals, poems, or anything else that speaks to you.

Supercharge your manifesting by lighting a yellow candle beside your moodboard during the new moon. Concentrate on the flame. Think about what inspires you and visualize the small changes that can make your moodboard self come to life. Hold these thoughts in your mind each time you add to your board.

Put your moodboard in the moon's light to charge. Turn to it whenever you need a little dose of your own magic.

IDENTITY AND BODY

—

Honoring (and Adoring) Your
Light, Dark, and Shadow

One of my closest friends, Laura, says that magic helped her fall in love with her body. In a *Luna Luna* article, she described a ritual for body acceptance in which she used food (kitchen witchery), self-love mantras, and gentle stretching to celebrate and honor her body. She was sick of feeling like she had to fit a mold or adhere to toxic beauty ideals propagated by a predatory culture.

Others have used rituals to find a home in their bodies after major surgery or being diagnosed with a chronic illness, or to protect themselves while walking down the street. In magic, there is autonomy—and the ability to reclaim your sense of power and spirit. This is especially so for marginalized bodies, bodies that aren't represented in media or advertisements, bodies that are objectified, ignored, or exoticized.

The spells, rituals, and practices in this section are designed to inspire you to take a holistic and celebratory approach to who you are—physically, emotionally, spiritually, and ancestrally. Please feel free to modify an action or incantation if something doesn't feel quite right to you—we all have different levels of comfort, so let your autonomy guide you in your magic-making efforts.

Use your journal to make notes as you go. Some ideas might be:

- Do I feel pressured to look a certain way?
- Do I feel pressured to feel a certain way about my body or others' bodies?
- What can I do to show myself love and acceptance?
- What would it look like if I stopped judging myself?
- What can I do to encourage body positivity and identity inclusivity among my peers?
- Am I treating others as they would like to be treated?
- What forms of magic make me feel good about myself and who I am?
- What can I do to carry that magic with me throughout the day and share it with others?

A Practice for Getting Comfortable with a Workout or Physical Health Routine

Our bodies are our armor, our story, our survival, our creativity, our home. But they are also vulnerable—to the messages we hear daily (many of them ableist) about how they should look and fit and work and take up space. It's no wonder that any body ritual we take part in—and going to the gym or playing a sport, doing physical therapy, or even meditating daily is a ritual—can be anxiety-inducing.

Working with the body is a loaded activity—one associated with everything from self-care and ideas of worth to physical health and body shame. And for anyone who has a disability, bodywork has its own set of challenges. With this practice, you'll be able to tap into your body and its abilities without an overly simple saying like "I love myself, and now everything is amazing." Because it's not always roses.

Materials

Your journal

Something to write with

Before you head to the gym, pool, doctor's office, the field, or anywhere else you do bodywork—make a list of what your body is already capable of doing. Do this in your magical journal. You might include:

- Stretching every morning
- Biking to work
- Running three miles a day
- Learning to navigate in a wheelchair
- Swimming for pain relief
- Rebuilding strength after surgery

Think about these capabilities while you use your body. Seriously: What a beautiful and capable engine you are.

When you finish your activity, turn to your journal again. Write about it. How did it make you feel: Strong? Sexy? Vulnerable? Alive? Free? Did the practice strengthen some of the things you're proud of doing? Did you learn something new? Take time to hone in on the positive and reward yourself for your efforts, even if it wasn't easy. Honor those feelings. This is about you feeling comfortable with you.

A Spell for Saying
Hell No to Labels

The world has a way of simplifying and reducing things into easy-to-digest parts—but more often than not, those parts serve only to divide us, to drain us of our color, beauty, and inner wild. We don't need to adhere to what people want us to be. And while some of us may know this instinctively, it's hard to put into practice, especially if you're not in a receptive community or safe space.

This spell will help you say no to binding labels, even if you are not in a position to dye your hair purple or quit wearing dresses or kiss who you want to kiss without repercussions. Of course, a spell can only do so much, so please do see a therapist or a respectful and confidential support group for additional help.

Materials

A piece of paper

Something to write with

A mirror of any size

A power object—something that represents who you are, like a shirt, a wig, makeup, a book, a photograph

A fireproof bowl

A sink

Matches or a lighter

You can perform this spell anytime, though it works best during the full moon, when energies are high and going deep is the only way.

On a piece of paper, write out a list of things (a.k.a. labels) that you feel pressure to be (e.g., overachiever, straight, feminine, quiet, skinny) but aren't and don't want to be.

Stand before your mirror with your power object and gaze at yourself. Honor all that you are. Say:

I am who I am in power and in love,
in storm and sky, in times then and now.

Set your things-you-aren't list in your fireproof bowl in the sink and burn it. Meditate on saying good-bye to those labels as the fire burns.

A Practice for Growing
Love for Nature

As a New Yorker, the closest I get to nature is the local park or garden (okay, it's more like the occasional subway rat). It takes determination for me to spend time in nature, although it's important to me that I do. I once traveled to a tropical region where there were a lot of bugs—a lot. Frightened, I felt disconnected and dispirited (and ashamed!). I needed to find a way to balance my love and respect for nature with my fear, without feeling bad for how I felt. Regardless of your fear—be it of lightning, dogs, or ants—this practice will help you tap into your connection with nature (although I recommend a therapist to help you with your specific fear).

Materials

An altar space

A candle

Essential oil

A bowl of water

A stone from outdoors, found that day

A small indoor plant (or outdoor plant you can bring indoors) that must be tended to

Set up your altar of earthly wares. Light a candle, mix some essential oil in a bowl of water, and wash your hands in the bowl. Hold the stone and tend to your little plant. Think, as you do it, about how the water feels, how the stone feels. Thank the water for cleansing you. Stare into the candle's flame.

Think about how nature affects you—how the moon controls the tides, how weather affects your mood, how the day goes from bright to dark to allow you to sleep.

Perform this each time you feel disconnected from nature—especially if you feel like you want to be connected to nature, rather than fear it.

A Confidence Spell for Public Speaking

We can thank the Greeks for the term "glossophobia"—which is a blending of *glōssa* (tongue) and *phobos* (phobia). The lovely sounding word may roll off your tongue like a dream—until you're tongue-tied at a public-speaking event. And since when has imagining your coworkers naked ever made anything easier?

Get a head-start by performing this spell the night before you need to give a speech, or a few days before a new job. It helps you conjure confidence by programming a magical power object that will give you a boost on the big day.

Materials

An orange candle (orange candles generally symbolize confidence and intellect)

A charm of some sort—a crystal, a small toy, a necklace

First, light your candle. Look into the flame and start talking aloud, completing these sentences:

I'm proud of . . .
I felt strong and capable when I . . .
People love me because I'm . . .

Focus on the good stuff. Do you make people laugh? Are you an amazing poet? Did you land the job? Are you charismatic? Let these self-compliments slip off your tongue and bask in their glory; sing your own praises, and swim through your sea of self.

When you're feeling good, take out your power object and hold it above the flame. Say:

I program this object to store all of my voice, confidence, and magic. It will help me sing.

A Self-Love Spell for Those
with Chronic Illness

If you, like me, are one of the 117 million people who lives with a chronic or debilitating illness, you may know how hard it can be to fully accept that you are sick. It's easy to wonder "Why me?" when pain becomes too much to bear or when you've spent weeks convincing your doctors that, yes, you're actually in pain.

Although professional medical care should be your first line of defense, this spell can help you send some love to your body, especially on those awful days.

Materials

A small pink candle

A piece of paper

Something to write with

An envelope or a sachet bag

Fireproof bowl

Matches or a lighter

Sink

In a comfortable space for you, burn a small pink candle (pink symbolizes love). Look into the flame and ask it to help you find acceptance. Take a few deep breaths and envision a white sparkling light surrounding and moving through your body. Send it to any body parts or pain points that need it.

Next, on a piece of paper, write a few lines of acceptance to your body. My personal favorite: "I may be sick, but I'm still a badass." You can also make a list of what is strong and reliable about your body. I love to conjure poet May Swenson's piece "Question," which reads: "Body my house / my horse my hound."

Next, say out loud:

Body, I accept you, even when it hurts.

Continue sending light throughout your body. Think about loving and accepting your body, including your illness. You may find it hard to do this, which is normal. It's not an easy process, but give it a try.

Put the note you wrote into an envelope or sachet bag. Sleep with it under your pillow—then throw it away or burn it inside in a fireproof bowl in your sink. Let the smoke imbue your words with its energy.

A Night-to-Day Ritual to Embrace and Celebrate Your Narrative

Sometimes we go through dark periods. Sometimes we find ourselves in someone else's dark period. Our lives are punctuated by loss and trauma—but they're often also glittering with resiliency and hope. It can be tempting to forget everything, to leave our wounds behind and not take a moment to appreciate any growth that may have come from them.

When I was a young, on the verge of tenth grade, I found myself in the foster care system—alone, without my family, without closure, without time to process. I worked hard to make sure I seemed "normal," happy, likable. Inside, I was a volcano, explosive, molten, angry. It took me years to make peace with my narrative, my truth. In fact, it was buried so deeply—muted, reduced to no-big-deal—that I rarely took the time to honor it. It was, after all, what made me me— what gave me the need for ritual, light, hope, self-care.

This ritual, which is half-completed at night and half-completed the following day, can help you honor your narrative, too, and shed any shame or stigma attached to it—whatever it may be.

Materials

A piece of paper

Something to write with

A small stone from outdoors

A small box to house the stone

Soil, shredded paper, or dried flower petals (enough to cover the stone)

The Night Ritual

First, tell your story. Write it down, get it out, pour it onto paper. What happened? What hurts? What haunts you? Who are you? Why does your narrative matter? How has it made you you?

Next, put your stone into the small box and cover it with the soil, paper, or dried flowers. Fold your paper into the box, as well. This is the symbolic representation of your silenced narrative. Ground yourself by meditating on what it means to silence that part of yourself—and what it might be like to honor it, even if it's painful.

The Day Ritual

The next day, wake up and open the box. Take the paper out. Remove and discard all of the filling. Lay the stone and your paper on the windowsill, in the light. You are unearthing your truth, showering it in light, and letting it breathe and exist. You are honoring it, and loving yourself in spite of or because of it.

A Glamour Ritual for Embracing Your Unique Beauty

There's a distinct difference between beauty and glamour. Beauty is often associated with the surface: It's every skin color, every shape, every breakout, every freckle, every hairstyle, every crooked tooth, every blushing cheek, every lash, and every eye color from the saffron-glinted black to the brown to the electric violet.

In my Mediterranean family, our beauty is thick, frizzy dark hair and long noses and wide hips. But our glamour is something else: It's our strong presence, our determination, our humor, our intensity. Sure, glamour can be your smile and the way you narrow your eyes, but it's more than that—it's the unnameable energy that spills from you, the way you light up when you feel free and alive, the way your perfume settles and intoxicates everyone in your path.

This gender-neutral glamour ritual helps you embrace your entire presence—that glittering you-ness that oozes from the inside out.

Materials

An altar space

Things you love (e.g., rose petals, seashells, perfume, your favorite decorations, figurines, crystals, candles, jewelry, fabric)

A mantra of your choosing

A photograph of yourself

First, choose a mantra. This might include:

I love my mysterious personality.

I am an intoxicating presence.

I am bathed in sensuality.

I am charming and witty.

My smile is disarming.

I am seen for my inner and outer beauty.

I am a magnetic force.

I inspire when I walk into the room.

Decorate your altar with the things you love. Use rose petals, crystals, glitter, small cacti—whatever feels like you. As you decorate your altar, repeat your mantra, letting it flow off your tongue as a song. In the very middle, place your photograph. This is a devotional to you. Gaze at your photograph and feel your words; they are casting a spell, creating a truth, and serving as a reminder.

GLAMOUR MEANS MANY THINGS:

· Your sensual, sidelong stare

· The way scent clings to your warm skin

· The very thing that makes you look unique

· The qualities you inherited from your parents

· Your hair in all its natural glory

· The way you glow when you laugh

· The presence you assert when you walk into a room

· What lovers and friends have said they adored about you

· What you love about yourself

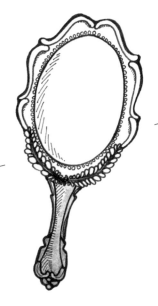

A Glamour Ritual to Boost Your Personal Power

Using lipstick as magic is a way of glamouring, and this ritual will help you feel like your most powerful self. Swap out the lipstick for chapstick, if you prefer. The goal of this ritual is to make you feel good, not necessarily to change the way you look (although that can be part of it).

Color Messages

If you're using lipstick, think about what its color means to you (and to the world at large). Red is classic and always stunning. Blue is unique and bold and daring. Black is dark and striking. Violet is magical and intuitive. These colors may mean different things to you, so let that guide you. Do you feel most confident when wearing blue lipstick? Do you feel most yourself in red? Does violet scream "get things done" to you? That's what you're looking to tap into.

Chapstick and Gloss

Maybe you prefer the simple ritual act of applying something that can "turn on" your power. While lipstick may message something to others, this ritual is mostly about you and how you feel when you wear it, so sheer chapstick or gloss will also do the trick.

Materials

Lipstick or chapstick

A small keychain knife

Set your chosen lip color or chapstick in front of you. Perform a moment of grounding; think about what you want the lipstick or chapstick to convey. You'll be programming it with that message, feeling, and mood.

Use the knife to draw a tiny, not-super-deep "x" into your lipstick or chapstick. State your intentions. For example, say:

With this color, this paint, this armor, I become myself strong and myself enchanted.

Now, carry the tube with you or keep it in a sacred space. Wear it when you need its power.

An Altar-Building Practice to Honor Your Ancestors

There are many reasons to build an altar for your ancestors, both recent and ancient. You may want to pay tribute to or simply acknowledge the family members who sacrificed everything for future generations, crossed wild seas without money or a place to go, or died by the hands of oppressors. You may want to make peace with a complex part of your family history, or honor those you never met but feel a blood-deep connection to culturally or spiritually. Whatever the case, your ancestors are part of your narrative, and this practice will help you create the altar space to connect with your family.

As a ritualized practice, this may be part of an ongoing activity dedicated to your ancestry. You may spend years collecting family mementos and stories, or building a narrative from ancestry records, if you are so fortunate as to have these. Erect an altar on a birthday or during a season or month that is particularly important to you.

Materials

A space to set up your altar

Items to decorate your altar

A piece of paper

Something to write with

First, choose items that represent your family heritage. They might include:

- Family pictures
- Family heirlooms
- Hand-me-downs
- Clothing
- Birth and death dates
- Pictures of a country or region or city where your ancestors came from
- Foods, spices, herbs, or flowers native to the area where your ancestors came from

Design and decorate your altar. Then sit and write a letter to your ancestors. You may want to forgive them, thank them, send them love, send them healing, say that you're sorry for their suffering, ask them to watch over you, or simply acknowledge their existence. Whatever your beliefs are, this sort of symbolic gesture can be a powerful tool for honoring and understanding your identity.

A Sex Magic Ritual for Manifesting Body Acceptance

Sex magic is sometimes wildly misunderstood, seen as simply driven by maniacal, hedonistic pleasure. While pleasure is phenomenal—of course—sex magic is less totally wild and more straight-up potent. Well-rooted in the fabric of history, sex magic is one of the most potent forms of magic that can be performed—alone or with a partner or partners.

You've likely heard of tantra or tantric sex. Tantras were fifth-century esoteric Hindu texts that suggested the body could be a spiritual tool. Tantras have a fascinating and complex history, and it's one that I recommend researching in-depth. For us, using sex magic means becoming or tapping into that spiritual tool—using our sexual energy to manifest or focus our intentions. It's not about performative sex or even feeling sexy; it's literally about taking that engine of energy our body revs and shaping out a direction for it.

In this ritual, we'll focus on using our own sexual energy to evoke feelings of body love and acceptance.

Materials

Your bed

Optional:

A mirror

A sex toy

On a night when you're alone—perhaps during the full moon, when energies are blazing and the magnificent vibrations are roiling through the cosmos—get ready to get cozy, settle in, and touch yourself in a way that gives you pleasure. Situate a mirror near the bed. If it feels uncomfortable to watch yourself, you can skip this; that discomfort may be good for some of us, since it's often through discomfort that we grow, but this is your choice.

Focus on your breath and the sensation. Follow them in your mind as they ebb and flow, as your physical sensations change with your touch.

Take a moment to honor your body, to send it love, to appreciate it. Look into the mirror, if you're using it, and celebrate yourself.

Climax is usually the goal in sex magic: to harness that grand boil-over of energy and, in the moment, use it to manifest your will. If you do climax, think or speak your intention. For example:

I will love my body and will treat it with respect.

Or

I accept my body as it is.

If you cannot or do not reach climax, focus heavily on your intention as you touch yourself.

Don't scold yourself or feel bad if your mind drifts away. This is a practice, not a one-time experience.

A Mirror Spell for When you Forget How Magical You Are

There are always going to be days when you feel less than divine, as though your spark, your magic, your intuition, and your drive have vanished into the abyss. You may feel empty, lackluster, or hungry for something more, some sense of ability or confidence—and you're coming up short.

This spell is especially useful in times when you've let yourself go—when self-care has become a distant memory, and you can't remember the last time you did anything for yourself (except showered, maybe). In this spell, you'll grease the magical gears, look inward, and find a pathway toward your own light. It's not a one-stop shop, of course, but it's a first step. (Remember not to be hard on yourself; you are an ocean, ebbing and flowing.)

Materials

Music that you have a strong connection to that also makes you feel empowered (If you can't hear music, try another sensory item, like wearing a soft fabric that you love, or spritzing your favorite perfume)

A mirror

Optional: A resurrection plant (also known as a rose of Jericho—they can be purchased from some occult or flower shops), placed in a bowl of water

Paper and pen

A prize (e.g., a snack, vibrator, lavender bubble bath, bouquet of roses, glass of wine)

Play your music, loud enough to drown out other sounds. Set the mirror before you, so you can gaze at yourself. If you have a resurrection plant, now would be a good time to water it or set it before you as you focus.

Ground yourself in the moment by simply being there, listening to the music, feeling the emotional connection to it, remembering why it means so much to you. Acknowledge the time you are taking for you. Breathe in and out, and accept the fact that you've been feeling less than lustrous lately—but that that will all change . . . now. Believe it.

Gaze into the mirror and find in yourself a friend, someone you love, someone you have been with your whole life. Allow feelings of blame, shame, or negativity to come right in and pass through. Say the following (or amend the language to fit your needs):

I see a powerful witch who won't take shit.
I see a powerful witch who will not fail.
I see a powerful witch who evolves and transforms.
I see a powerful witch who will prevail.

Repeat this three times while looking in the mirror. Afterward, envision clear ways that your life can be more magical: Are you writing more often? Do you take more time to visit nature? Say those ideas or practices out loud. Scream them over the music, if you want to.

Next, make a list of those ideas. Fold the paper and place it in your bag so that you carry it with you, or keep it on your desk.

Next, get up and treat yourself, witch! Focus on the pleasure, on the beauty, on the richness of the experience. Be you, wholly and fully; experience the delight of existing in your own magic, whatever that means to you.

A Poppet Practice
for Body Love

A poppet, in magic, is a doll or an item that represents someone's likeness. You may make a simple poppet for body love—so that you can send love to yourself, work through a time of illness, work on self-esteem, or remove negativity surrounding you.

Materials

2 large pieces of felt (at least the size of a book)

Chalk

Scissors

Needle and thread

Cotton or fabric scraps

Optional:

· Stapler

· Pins

· Branches

· Yarn

To make a fabric poppet, lay the two pieces of felt on top of one another. Fold them in half vertically. Use the chalk to outline one half of a body on one side of the felt. With the felt still folded in half, use the scissors to cut along the outline of the body. Unfold the felt—you should have two complete bodies. Use a needle and thread to sew the poppet together, stuffing it with cotton or fabric as you progress. If you don't know how to sew, staple or pin the pieces of felt together.

Alternatively, you may make a poppet from branches or sticks, using yarn to hold it together in the shape of a body.

No matter your medium, adorn your poppet, speak to it, or carry it with you as you please. You may:

· Adorn it with beads

· Write short love letters to yourself and leave it with the doll

· Surround it with flowers

· Create an altar for your poppet and bring it offerings or gifts daily

· Speak to it in confession

· Surround it with healing herbs

· Sew a magical piece of programmed fabric to it to represent healing or self-love or confidence

· Sleep with it

· Treat it as you want to be treated

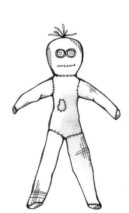

A Monthlong Lunar Practice for
Self-Understanding

For those of you who love to work with the moon, this practice is the ultimate lunar goodie. It will help you track your mood, understand yourself, determine which areas of your life need extra love or support, and find ways to increase joy. It's also just fun.

Materials

Paper

Something to write with

A mason jar

Optional: Decorations (e.g., crystals, flowers, shells, or other small decorative items)

Start this practice at the new moon. At the end of each day, write on a single piece of paper your daily mood and the day's lesson: What did you learn? What did you realize? What do you need to focus on? You may also track specific things (e.g., creativity, self-esteem, health, energy levels). On the back of the paper write down the moon phase.

Place this in a mason jar (which you can beautify by filling it with crystals or flowers or shells) and keep this at the window under moonlight—your goal here is to really connect with Luna.

At the end of the entire moon cycle (by the time the moon reaches its new phase again, moving from waxing to full to waning to new), you'll have tracked an entire cycle's worth of self.

Empty your mason jar. Lay out each piece of paper and write, in your grimoire, what you learned. You may see patterns emerge, so start connecting the dots with how your feel and the phases of the moon. Are you more imaginative during the full moon? Integrating the moon's cycles into your life may help you get in tune with yourself and nature.

Practices to Help You Derive Power from Your Period

Not every woman has a period, but those who do know the labyrinthine pathways of its reckoning. Some women never get used to its mental and physical demands, while others think of it as beautiful or empowering. If you get a period—especially if you deal with an extremely painful or mind-of-its-own cycle—these practices can:

- Help you reclaim your body from the pain, inconvenience, expense, and social stigma around periods, blood, and "you must be on your period" comments

- Help you make peace with chronically complicated or frustratingly painful periods

- Let you tap into your innate power and capability

- Rename what it means to be a goddess: messy, real, flawed, annoyed, tired, powerful

Materials

None

Period Power Practices

Practice 1. Use your period blood to power a spell by dabbing a little bit of it on a candle you're using. Witches have long used period blood to kick up a spell's potency, since many believe it represents the body's power. This power isn't related only to giving birth but also to handling pain and emotional discomfort.

Practice 2. Keep a journal of period moods, dreams, and powers. Do you feel more intuitive? Do you dream more? What are your dreams telling you?

Practice 3. Invoke an archetype during your period—someone who represents strength, power, or femininity (if you identify with that)—and do some work around what they symbolize. Meditate on their being and infuse your daily life with thoughts or ideas they might represent.

Practice 4. Because your body is getting rid of something during your period, you might choose to do a good-bye spell.

Practice 5. Take a bath and pamper yourself. Water is an emotional element, so if you're experiencing a particularly difficult period, treat yourself to a bubble bath filled with rose petals and salts.

Practice 6. Have a party. I call these moon parties, since the moon controls the tide. Invite all of your friends over to celebrate, drink fizzy things, watch melodramatic movies, sing loudly, and try on all your clothes. Train yourself to think of your period as a time for fun, rather than a time for fear.

Practice 7. Manifest with the pain. Lie in bed and feel the feelings. You may find a beautiful sense of power blooming within you if you choose to use the pain to manifest. Acknowledge the pain and ride its wave as you lie there. Use the energy, much like you would in sex magic, to manifest an intention.

Practice 8. Work on your healing prowess. Get comfortable, breathe deeply but normally, and send light to your womb. Say:

I send you, body, light and love.

Practice 9. Help support legislation to make employers offer free tampons to employees. Support and fight for legislation that strips men from their power over the female body.

A Ritual for Building Empathic Powers and Connecting with Others

Because witchcraft is so closely tied to social and political awareness, you may feel the need to build on that empathy—especially when times are tough and you feel tapped out. Living in a time of political chaos and social crisis is all about balance: resist, recalibrate, and repeat. Inevitably, there will be days when your heart feels numb and the darkness seems to seep in to do its dirty work. But darkness, in many ways, can be good; it ups our ante, teaches us to envision new paths for the future, brings us together, and allows us to look inward. In this ritual, you will actively tap into all of that so you can be there for yourself and for others.

Materials

A bed, chair, or yoga mat (somewhere comfortable!)

Rose quartz

Get comfortable and breathe deeply, in and out, until you feel at ease, receptive, and calm. Place the rose quartz on your chest, over your heart, or hold it gently in your hand. Envision the crystal radiating warm, rose-colored light, and passing its glow into you and over you.

Say:

Empathy fills my every word and touch.

Repeat this statement until you feel it—until you feel that you've truly replenished your stock, if you will. This may take a few tries, and that's okay. Repeat this ritual as often as needed.

ARE YOU AN EMPATH?

According to Judith Orloff, MD, a psychiatrist, intuitive healer, empath, and author of *The Empath's Survival Guide: Life Strategies for Sensitive People*, empaths are people who can sense subtle energies (e.g., energy fields or vibrations, or prana—which in Hindu philosophy is our life force). Empaths absorb these energies from other people or even environments, animals, and nature. Those energies can become deeply entwined with the empath's own, to the point of becoming totally fused—which can be magnificent for healing or detrimental to the empath.

Empaths:

- Require alone time to defragment
- Often feel overstimulated quite easily
- Have aversions to loud noises or intense smells
- Deeply feel transitions between places and activities
- Often want to help others, and can be relied upon for deep comfort and understanding—frequently leading to their own discomfort

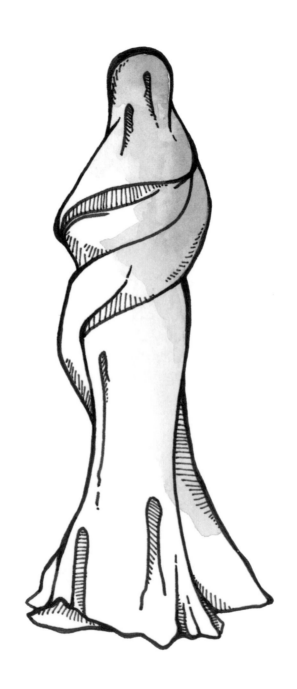

SHADOW WORK

Honoring Darkness and
Finding Light in the Shadows

Darkness isn't a vacuum one can avoid entirely, nor is it necessarily a bad thing. In it, there is truth and growth and potent self-actualization. Our shadow selves want to be seen and heard—but delving into their subterranean caverns requires work. These practices help us forge a path through (and beside) the darkness, lighting embers along the way.

As children, we were much more comfortable living in that liminal space. We could believe in goblins and faeries and other-worlds; we were tapped into the goings-on of things beyond our sight.

As we grew up, a sort of binary assortment took place. Suddenly things become real or not real, bad or good. In fact, we're taught to believe that we should fear what we don't understand.

By now, you've probably cast a few spells and tried your hand at some of the practices in this book. If you feel a little more comfortable with your inner power, then you can use this section to gaze into the dark for answers, confront parts of yourself that you've hidden, and identify archetypes to indulge your shadow self.

Women and femmes in particular are taught that we are only valuable when we are good and happy and bright and easy to talk to. But we can have darkness and nuance and complexity and a little bit of madness. We can be multilayered, we can move between the layers, and we can indulge in the underbelly if we want to.

No matter your belief system or what you've been taught to discard as mythos and madness, you end up seeing a lot more when you wander into the dark. But let it be known that darkness cannot exist without light, and vice versa. They are interwoven, flowing like water around and through one another.

As they say, *in darkness, light.*

A Red Rose Ritual for
Aging Acceptance

There's no way to erase social pressures around aging, especially when it comes to women and femmes; the beauty ideals are brutal, unhealthy, and toxic, and no spell or ritual can change that. But accepting that we all grow, age, and eventually leave this earth is one way we can take back the beauty narrative and our own response to the toxicity.

Maybe you don't feel those pressure, though. Maybe you feel only love and excitement about the future and your body and your skin, and their beautiful, natural changes. Whatever the case, this ritual will help you honor and confront aging changes, both in the short term and in a more existential way.

Materials

A white candle

A mirror

Tape or ribbon

A single, natural, undyed red rose free of formaldehyde and chemicals

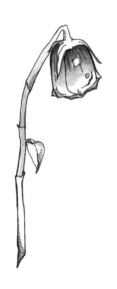

Light your candle and sit with it before you. Gaze into the mirror and look upon yourself. Speak aloud some of the things you notice:

I accept my eye color.
I accept the way my skin wrinkles when I
  smile.
I accept my freckles.
I accept my natural hair.
I accept my sun spots.

Hang the single rose upside down—tape it to a wall or use a small ribbon to tie it up somewhere. Look at its beauty and admire its shape, color, and scent.

For the next few days, watch the rose decay. Observe its changes: the way it curls inward and loses shape, the way its color deepens or fades. Spend time thinking about the processes of nature, and of how you, as a natural being, fit into that cycle. See how the rose is not the same—and yet the same; still beautiful, but different.

A Ritual for Getting Comfortable
with the Shadows

Many people believe that our shadow selves hold the key to understanding our true nature. So why not peer into the abyss and find it for yourself? (Sound easy? It's not: Shadow work is the hardest work to do, and many people resist it because it's uncomfortable.)

This ritual will help you confront that darkness, which might take the form of bloodlust, possessiveness, or extreme fear. With my shadows, I have worked on my intense need for approval from others. It's not something I like about myself, but gazing into it has been helpful, and I've learned to recognize when I'm doing it.

You'll want to set aside about an hour, in the evening, for this ritual.

Materials

Three black candles

Something to write with

Your shadow journal

Sit in a dark room and light three black candles—preferably near a wall so it can catch the shadows' dance. You may want to envision a circle of safety around you. Take several deep breaths and know that you are in control. You can stop this ritual at any time. Watch the flames move—they represent that feeling of jealousy, or a messed-up idea you have about a friend, or a negative stereotype you hold that you want to confront.

Watch the shadow move, talk to it, ask it questions, and ask it to transmute your negativity into something else, something you can work with and learn from. Think about ways you can dismantle whatever it is that haunts you. You may not have a clear answer. If your mind wanders, just breathe and come back to your focus. Write your ideas down in a shadow journal.

When you're finished, blow out the candles, watching the shadows leave. Ground yourself by taking a moment to notice the here and now. It may take several sessions before you come to terms with the shadow—be patient with yourself.

SHADOW WORK

Any book about light would be remiss not to mention the overwhelming importance of working with the shadow. Shadow work is a kind of magic that requires you to tap into the dark, constructively. The shadow, according to psychiatrist C. G. Jung, is something dark, something we keep hidden, silent, or tucked away. Often the shadow is part of our subconscious. It doesn't have to be negative, necessarily, but people often associate it with something they need to work on. Shadow work is done differently throughout many traditions, but it's essentially the practice of identifying and even accepting those latent, hidden parts of ourselves. (This is, in essence, a form of therapy as well.)

In witchcraft, it's important to be grounded and clearheaded before working with the shadow, since it can be triggering, especially if you're already dealing with health or mental health issues. Often, shadow work can be done through journaling, memory work (sifting through old memories and visions to get to the root of something), or by simply being mindful of the shadow as you go about your day. There's no end or beginning; it's a process that you'll come back to again and again—so be patient with yourself!

A Spell to Summon Your Inner Hecate

The Greek goddess of magic and in-between spaces, Hecate is all about ghosts and portals and crossroads. Hecate herself led Demeter into the underworld. She is also a common representation of the Crone, or the third stage of a woman's life.

In this spell, you will use Hecate as your guide—to shrug off the fabric of the day and step into the cloak of darkness, to trespass into shadow territory. This spell can be used to:

- Pass a message to the dead
- Come to terms with death or dying
- Meditate on a deep, dark truth you hold
- Contemplate or ideate on a journey you will take

Perform this spell on the night of a dark moon or a new moon.

Materials

A gray candle

A key to be used solely for this spell

Ground yourself and light your candle. Hold the key in your left palm. Gaze at the flame and ask Hecate to guide you into the darkness. Envision the key opening a portal between what you can see and what you cannot: other realms, the underworld, shadow spaces. Envision yourself walking into a dark space. Let the door close behind you. Stand in the darkness and focus on your intent: to talk to the dead, contemplate death, meditate on your dark truth. Do not leave the room until you feel a resolution. Once you do, open your eyes, snuff out the candle, thank Hecate, and bury or dispose of the key.

A Practice for Finding Your
Shadowy Archetype

Have you ever been attracted to a character, goddess, femme fatale, villain, or bad boy? Yeah, we all have. It's complex because we're taught what's right and what's wrong, and we never want to be on the wrong side of an issue.

This ritual will let you explore that shadowy archetype—not simply because it's fun but also because there's something to be gained by it. These dark characters are the very representation of parts of ourselves: They're confident, bossy, creative, no-bullshit, and sexual. They've disregarded the boundaries of what's good and acceptable and clean. And they speak to parts of ourselves that we rarely mention out loud. This ritual will help you identify that shadow figure and incorporate aspects of their personality into your life.

Materials

Your shadow journal

Something to write with

A picture of your shadow archetype

Think about your shadow archetypes. Pick one to focus on.

In your shadow journal, write about what you like about them (and what you don't).

Think about small ways that their qualities could play out in your life. Can you ask more often for exactly what you want? Do you want to stop accepting no for an answer? Do you want to up your glamour because it makes you feel powerful? Do you want to stop giving a shit about glamour altogether? Do you want to learn tai chi? Do you want to get to the finish line, no matter what?

Keep a picture of your shadow archetype in your bag or purse. Turn to it when you need to indulge in their dark wisdom.

A Ritual to Confront and Resolve
Cognitive Dissonance

Often, aspects of our lives contradict our morals, ethics, and pleasures. It could be that you work for a company you despise, or that you wear oodles of expensive, fancy leather goods but secretly feel this goes against your beliefs around animal cruelty. This is cognitive dissonance, and it can split a hole in your soul the size of Hades. Sometimes it's hard to resolve: You need a paycheck, so you can't quit the job you hate. Sometimes, it's a little easier—but you have to take the time to make the change.

Here's where shadow work comes in handy. You'll use your shadow journal in this ritual to record instances of dissonance and brainstorm how to replace them with resonance.

Materials

A piece of paper

A fireproof bowl

Matches or a lighter

Your shadow journal

Start by grounding yourself. Ask yourself: What do I feel split about? What is the cause of my dissonance? Settle into your discomfort and go deep—don't accept surface answers or avoid the full, glaring intensity of the answer.

On a single piece of paper, write:

I feel cognitive dissonance about _____ because it makes me feel _____.

And then write:

To resolve this dissonance, here is what is in my power: _____.

After you've spent some real time going deep with these feelings, finish writing. Then burn the entries in your fireproof bowl. Afterward, write about the entire experience in your journal. How do you feel? Do you feel empowered? Uncertain? Why?

When you're done, take a few moments to send love to yourself for being conscious and willing to make needed changes.

A Practice for Building
Your Own Underworld

Does the title of the spell feel a little heavy, a little impossible? I couldn't tell you how to connect with the underworld in a real way, because we all have different beliefs. But this practice can help you create a symbolic connection to that place of death, darkness, and secrets. In this practice, you'll build your own underworld where you can go to grieve, when you want to get rid of something, or to store your negativity—for eternity, or even for a little while. It can be a place you visit regularly.

Materials

A mason jar with a screw-top lid

A handful of stones (obsidian or smoky quartz will do, too)

Whenever you have a dark thought—anger, grief, existential despair, hatred for your job, fear—you'll want to create a place for it, somewhere where it doesn't interfere with your everyday world. This place is inside your mason jar. It's your own little representation of the underworld.

Find a stone to represent a feeling you'd like to say good-bye to or bury or keep out of the light. Place it in your jar and say:

In my underworld, I place feelings of _____.

You might choose to place feelings of insecurity or grief in your underworld. Each time you put a stone into the jar, concentrate on pouring that energy in with it. Every stone that you place inside your jar is an encapsulation of those feelings or energies. Make sure you're able to close the lid tightly. When your underworld jar is full, cleanse the stones under the moon and start again.

A Santa Muerte Death and Rebirth Spell

Shedding our skin is natural and necessary, but that doesn't make it easy or even desirable. We often resist change, especially at times when we need it the most. But as a Scorpio, the sign of death or transformation, I often hunger for change and adaptation, to kill off the part of me that is no longer necessary and to conjure the part of me that needs to crawl out of its shell: codependence shed for self-love, anger shed for patience, fear shed for intuition, obsessive grief shed for peace of mind.

My good friend Leza Cantoral is a Mexican writer and a witch, and she performs a spell in the name of Santa Muerte (in Mexico, Santa Muerte is the personification of death itself) to aid in transformation and to accept the phases of life. Leza kindly allowed me to adapt her spell for this grimoire.

Materials

A black candle

Skull imagery

An offering of some sort (e.g., candy or a shot of liquor)

Something you can shed (e.g., a single strand of hair, an article of clothing, a piece of jewelry you can remove)

Begin by creating an altar. Light your candle, position your skull imagery, and make your offering. Leave this altar up for a week or more (just do not to leave the candle alight while you're not home). You want to spend some time with death and let its presence take up space.

When you are ready to start the spell, light your candle and remove something from yourself—a piece of hair, a nail clipping, your shirt. Place it on the altar.

Sit or lie down, as if dead—all while picturing Santa Muerte reviving you with light and love. Say:

Death is rebirth; I transform; I am reborn; I am darkness and I am light.

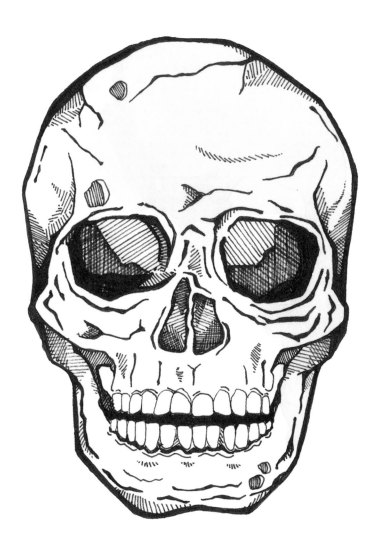

A Spell for Disposing of Serious Psychic Garbage

Has a negative idea been haunting you forever? Do you feel jealous of your friends or shameful about your finances? Do you feel worthless at work or in your relationships? Do you think of yourself as undeserving? Do you punish yourself for eating too much?

You know these ideas and feelings don't serve you—but they're in there, swirling around and creating a storm of silence and exhaustion and cyclical self-hatred. On the flip side, maybe these feelings have pushed us to succeed, to be more empathetic toward others. It's important to recognize that, even if you are disposing of the feeling.

Aside from speaking to a therapist, you can get to the root of the issue with shadow work. It's almost never easy, and sometimes it can be triggering—so read through this spell first to decide if it is right for you. Know that it might become an ongoing practice, one that you chip away at. Maybe you want to perform this on each new moon, just to give yourself the space and time to feel these feelings.

Materials

A black candle

A small object, like a button or a coin

Black yarn

Rose quartz

Light your candle. Quietly think about the feeling you'd like to let go. Really get down into the muck of it. Hold your small object in your open left palm. Imbue the object with those negative feelings. When you feel you've let it all out, take the yarn and mindfully wrap it around the object. Do this for as long as you can, until the object is totally encased in black yarn.

Once it is, say:

[Feeling or idea], you do not hold power over me.
I am more powerful than you.
I choose self-love and light.

Now, hold your rose quartz and envision it spreading love and light through your body. Dispose of the object as soon as you've snuffed out your candle.

A Ritual for Illuminating
Your Shadows

One of the most radical acts of magic is the act of self-honesty and naked vulnerability. This ritual is exactly that: It's designed to help you say hello to your shadows (things you don't want to think about or talk about often, events you don't have closure around, memories you bury) and bring them to light, literally.

If you are not comfortable yet with shadow work, save this for a time when you feel more able to confront your deeper truths. This ritual may leave you emotionally exhausted or even a bit off-balance right afterward, so be ready. In the end, this ritual will move your shadows from their depths to the surface, which ultimately can be a good thing. You have the control to summon whatever shadow you'd like. You may leave others in the underworld of your shadow space.

Materials

A shower or bath

Paper

Something to write with

Several small candles, with which to surround yourself in a circle (one for each of your shadows)

An obsidian or amethyst

Cleanse yourself in a bath or shower and sit naked (if you are comfortable with this) on a blanket on the floor or in a chair.

Write down your shadows on small pieces of paper, such as "My self-doubt," "Childhood memories of my mother," "Feeling inadequate at work," or "My shameful secret." Be explicit and specific.

Arrange the candles around you, unlit, in a circle, one for each shadow. Place each paper before the corresponding candle.

Sit in the middle, thoughtfully contemplating each shadow. Give each a moment; breathe into it and acknowledge it. You don't need to make peace or forgive—simply listen to its voice.

Light each candle. This is the symbolic act of bringing your shadows to the surface and finding strength in your own honesty.

To amp up this ritual, keep nearby an obsidian, which balances darkness and light, or an amethyst, which is used in meditation and raising consciousness.

A Practice for
Building Intuition

Intuition is a liminal thing—it's something we all have but that's influenced by any number of factors, like external pressures, learned responses, self-doubt, and a disconnect from the self or nature. But it's there, inside each of us, as a well of knowledge. It's in our fight-or-flight instinct; it's our gut feelings about a person; it's when we think about a person a moment before they call. (Does this happen all the time for you? That's your intuition working!)

This practice will help you tap into that—get down into the dark spaces and shadows where you've probably hidden your intuition (because we're taught it's not reliable or scientific or objective enough). Developing and learning to trust your intuition is integral to powering your magic.

For me, learning to listen to my intuition changed my life. It helped me make better choices about who I keep as friends, and helped me make major life decisions when I just "felt off" about something. And it is has never let me down. Here's how you can hone your intuition.

Materials

A candle

Amethyst

Paper

Something to write with

Set aside an hour to ground, meditate, and focus. Quiet all sounds. Light a candle.

Get into a comfortable position. Hold the amethyst in your hand or set it before you.

Close your eyes and focus on your breath. It's okay if your thoughts wander. Bring your attention back to your breath.

Imagine a long cord running from your spine down to the inner core of the earth. Feel the energy connecting you. Connect with the amethyst as well. Amethyst is commonly used (and beloved) for developing and strengthening psychic abilities, intuition, and visionary powers.

Think about something that you're curious about or worried about. Is there someone you feel unsure about? Is there a life move you're hesitating to make? Ask yourself: What does your gut tell you?

Swim in that gut feeling for a few moments. Write it down on paper.

Do this practice a few times per week to develop your intuition. Keep tabs on how the feelings unfold and what you might be right about.

Developing and learning to trust your intuition is integral to powering your magic.

WRITING MAGIC

———

Making Page Magic with Spellcraft and Journaling

Your word is your wand. That's not just a pretty idea; it's the truth. Language runs the world, forms the foundation for learning, enables us to understand and feel compassion for one another, and allows us to tell the stories that literally change the world. It may be one of the most powerful forms of magic we have; from the powerful sounds of sacred chanting to the intentional, thoughtful rhyming patterns of elaborate spells, how we use our language—and what that language means—matters. What you write becomes a time stamp, a declaration, an intention, and a living, breathing magical vehicle.

When you sign off on a letter, you have a choice: You could write "sincerely," "thank you," "love," "best regards," "xoxo." Each has its own meaning, which changes according to your intent and the letter's recipient. When you text someone an emoji—the crystal ball, the wilted rose, the dancing woman in the wild red dress—you're conveying a specific energy, a message under the message, an implication that can be felt and understood in its subtlety and specificity.

The same goes for when you overhear someone saying something cruel or degrading to another human being. Your body can feel it. It's not just the intention; it's the word's energy, lingering out there in the world, poisoning everything around it. Words—single words, uttered toward whole communities of people—have the power to oppress and spread suffering. Those words can also be reclaimed as tools of empowerment. Those words can bring down regimes. Those words can build cultures and forge communities.

While your silent intentions hold potency, the word—on the page, written down for good—kicks your magic into overdrive.

A Practice for Writing about Someone Who Has Passed Away

As Chilean novelist Isabel Allende wrote in her magnificent book *Eva Luna*, "There is no death . . . People die only when we forget them . . . If you can remember me, I will be with you always."

The idea that our memory is part of the elixir of immortality is powerful—imbuing us with the ability to keep someone's spirit alive and close. Use this practice if you have to write a eulogy, share a message about a loved one who has passed on, are writing about the life of someone lost, or simply want to revisit your memories of someone. Getting details down can allow us to move on in a small way; we won't fret about whether we'll forget the person. We can always draw on what we've written, fall into the tiny details, or read through the pages on their birthday or anniversary of their death.

Materials

Your journal

Something to write with

Use your journal to list out every memory you have about them—go wild with the details: their oversized sweaters, their fondness for honey, the way their house always smelled like lilies and musk.

Next, write about things you did with them.

Write next about how they supported, inspired, or loved you. What did that feel like?

Last, write about ways they may have hurt you. Have you forgiven them, or is the hurt still fresh?

What would you like to tell them? Which memories do you want to keep alive? Which would you like to let go of, in peace and respect?

When you're done, speak each line. This may feel challenging, but casting your truth out loud—listening to your own words, sharing them with yourself—can help you find a sense of closure.

A Journaling Practice
for Taking Risks

Anaïs Nin, born in 1903, was a writer and diarist ahead of her time, and her works have been long beloved for their personal details. I read her whenever I need to look deep into the waters of self-exploration and honesty. To me, Nin's writing represents the risk we take when we allow ourselves to be ourselves.

For this activity, you will become a diarist like Nin—writing before you head off to work or start your day. Set aside thirty minutes to do this—just enough to breathe deeply and get your mind into a space of sharing. You might first head outside and soak up some light, or take a mindful shower. Or, you can sit silently in bed holding an amethyst, a powerful symbol of deeper self-understanding.

Materials

A dedicated notebook

Amethyst (optional)

Flower petals (optional)

Meditate on what's holding you back: Is it asking for a raise? Ending a toxic friendship? Applying to a dream job? Finally writing that book? Remember, while risk-taking is a necessary aspect of personal growth, your risk-taking should not hurt you or anyone else.

Without judgment, acknowledge your fears or any self-created obstacles. When you're ready, begin journaling. Write down some of the following ideas:

- What am I holding onto or holding back from?
- What is my goal or dream?
- What would happen if I took the risk? How would I feel?
- What is the first thing I can do to take a step forward?

Do this every morning for seven days. (Note to any nightlings: If you can't stomach the idea of writing anything before your morning coffee, you can do this before bed.) Focus on one risk or goal per session. Keep your diary somewhere beautiful, surround it with flowers, nurture it, decorate it. Creatively housing your ideas allows you to water them with energy— so be creative.

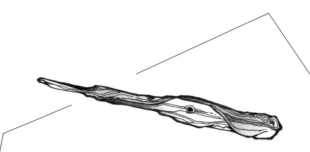

BEHIND THE SCENES:
WRITING YOUR OWN INCANTATION

An incantation is a magical statement or declaration used in spellwork. Writing your own is empowering. You can fill it with your favorite words and ideas. Color it in with what you need and want. Shape it with the sounds that make you swoon. Pay attention to the way the verbs make you feel. Are they actionable enough? Specific enough? Think about creating your own spells or cowriting a spell with a friend. You could create a bilingual spell or a spell-as-song.

To write an incantation:

- **Write it in the present.** Doing this allows you to believe it, and really inhabit the message of it.

- **Specify as best as you can.** The more specific you are, the better. You don't want the message or intent to be misinterpreted in any way.

- **Use your voice.** Are you a descriptive, lush writer? Do you prefer to keep it simple, clean, and short? Be you. Infusing your incantation with your authenticity gives your incantation power.

A Writing Spell
for Abundance

Every witch wishes they could simply manifest money—money to pay the rent, money to pay for health care, money to help others, money to start a company or build a home. But manifesting money straight up doesn't usually work. What does is casting a spell for abundance—in all forms: dreamy new opportunities, social network invitations that can help you advance in your career, the option to take part in a collaborative adventure. Hopefully, those new experiences and opportunities lead to money, stability, and growth. This spell will help you say the right words to attract the right sort of abundance.

Materials

A piece of paper

Something to write with

A bowl or jar

Coins

Start by writing down a line that invokes exactly the kind of abundance you're seeking. To avoid the universe interpreting your spell as "any sort of abundance will do," be specific—because you could find an amazingly well-paying job that leaves you absolutely miserable.

For example:

I have a well-paying job that makes me happy and fulfilled.

I have a ton of new opportunities that will bring me stability and enjoyment.

I make enough money by pursuing my interests and creative passions.

Next, say the line aloud. Then place the paper at the bottom of a jar or bowl. Cover it completely with coins—any type will do. Keep the container near your doorway to attract abundance. Feed it once a day—even if it's just a single coin. Say your phrase every single time.

A New Moon Crystal Practice for Daily Emotional Growth

For this daily practice, you'll supercharge your emotional wellness using both crystal magic and the sparkling light of the new moon.

For this practice, make sure you have three to five small crystals that represent emotional needs (e.g., vitality, love, protection). Part of this ritual is taking the time to source the right crystals for you, knowing that you're working toward an important well-being practice for yourself. (A list of crystals can be found on page 31.) Each crystal will help you manifest your emotional goals. You'll "grow" those emotional goals by the light of the moon; think of the moon as the way you'll water your goal, and think of the crystals as the soil helping it to grow. Begin this practice during a new moon.

Materials

A piece of paper

Three to five crystals

A window

Close your eyes and focus. Then open your eyes and write out your emotional goals on a piece of paper. For example:

I am full of love.
I am protected from outside negativity.
I am clear of mind and focused.

You choose—and be as specific as possible.

Next, lovingly place the corresponding crystal on top of your written goal. Set the papers and crystals in a windowsill, where the moon's light can charge them. Do this for as many nights as you need to, and carry the crystals with you each day.

A Writing Ritual to Lovingly
Sever Cords with Someone

The etheric body, according to esoteric philosophy, is considered a foundational layer of the aura or human energy field. It is connected to the physical body as well as to divine or other energies. Whether you prefer to view this as metaphorical or literal, the idea that our etheric bodies are connected to others via an etheric cord makes sense. Our experiences together, a person's words, our memories of someone—they all leave us covered in heavy, lasting energetic residue. Sometimes that residue is negative: angry, guilty, cruel, regretful, resentful. Sometimes you don't want to hold a space for those feelings anymore. You may not want to forget the person all together, but you want to get rid of the ghost of bad memories. You want to replace them with love, forgiveness, or, more simply, acceptance.

In this ritual, you'll sever that metaphorical cord and replace it with exactly what you need.

Materials

An object that represents what you'd like to disconnect from

A black cord, like yarn or string

Something to write with

A piece of paper

Scissors or a small knife

A bathtub

Favorite music

Lavender bath salts or rose quartz

Find an object that represents what you'd like to cut cords with, and bind yourself with it by tying it to your ankle or arm (just remember you'll need to use one hand to write with). Think about what you'd like to cut. Was it the person's toxic jealousy? Their narcissism or moodiness? Was it not something that they did but the toxicity you created together? Was it that what you had was intense and powerful but unsustainable? Don't use the person's name, but be specific. Focus on the feelings they left you with rather than the person as a whole. List the feelings you'd like to keep from them, as well. For example, you might write:

I sever the feelings of exhaustion and sadness caused by this relationship. I sever the control these feelings have over me. I leave behind only the happy memories.

Read your statement aloud, then cut yourself free from the physical cord.

Meditate on the physical and metaphorical cord being cut between yourself and the emotions caused by the other person—envision those feelings dissolving into calm, kind, understanding, glittering light.

Take a long bath. While you do, play your favorite music. Use lavender bath salts or bathe with a few rose quartzes in your hand. Imagine the toxicity, negativity, and hard feelings washing away. When you're ready, drain the tub. Dry off and see that connection washed away. Alternatively, in place of a bath, simply wash your hands and follow the practice above in just the same way.

Practices for Writing
Magical Poetry

There have long been poems about witchcraft and magical practices. In the sixteenth century, author Nicholas Breton wrote, "A witche, and not a witche, and yet a witche indeede." But there's something more beautiful than poems about magic: poems as magic.

What can a spell accomplish? What can a poem create? The intersection is in their intention. It's the combining of parts to make something altogether new—an emotion, a reaction, an action, or a decision. Spells and poems are unmeasurable, outside of time and the rules of language and perception.

Materials

Paper and pen

Here are some ways you can use poetry as magic:

Write during the phases of the moon. Infuse your poem with intention by tying it to the moon phases—write a manifestation poem during the full moon, a releasing poem during the waning moon. You can even charge a poem by the light of the moon to amp it up. Like an incantation or a mantra, read the poem any time to evoke the energy you seek.

Write your spells as poems. The words we write are magical. Language has always been at the core of spellcraft. Choosing your words with precision means you decide what the universe can interpret and what is defined, sought after, actualized, and manifested. It is a reclamation, an inner power.

Power up your poetic metaphors. A rose may symbolize love for some; to others, water might symbolize fluidity. In writing poetry, you decide your associations. If you build your spells out of poems, your language and vision are the ultimate forces.

Free-write. Free-writing, the act of writing from your unconscious, unhooks the creative gates, letting the shadow self come out to play. Don't be limited by self-editing. Free-write for a week each night before bed. See what themes and words emerge.

A Practice for Developing Your Own Grimoire

A grimoire is, essentially, a witch's diary. It's not exactly a diary of life events but a diary of magical practices, written spells, and results. Really, a grimoire is to each witch what it needs to be. Here's how to create your own.

Materials

A notebook, store-bought or handmade

A pen or pencil

First, you'll want to get (or make!) a notebook that speaks to you in its design and size. Let it find you. It doesn't have to be lined; it doesn't have to be leather-bound; it can be however you envision it. If you prefer, use a digital format. In your grimoire, you can include:

- A diary of spells performed—and their results
- Lists of magical tools and your associations with them (herbs, crystals, candles)
- Intuitions and psychic feelings
- Letters to the dead
- Drawings of sigils and symbols
- Records of how you feel after casting spells
- Dreams and messages from dreams
- Images that speak to your magical lifestyle
- Names of magical books you'd like to read

You can decorate and beautify your grimoire in lots of ways: Dab essential oils into the pages, include crushed flowers or dried leaves, draw images, tape pictures into it, or create pretty lunar calendars for the year.

An Embodiment-Writing Spell for Creating Your Dream

Setting your intention into reality—or at least giving your intention a fighting chance—is an integral part of magical work. One of the ways I like to manifest my intentions is through writing, in the present tense, what it is that I want to create. On my body. I like to use nontoxic ink to do this. (Please skip this spell if you have very sensitive skin.)

With this spell, you will literally embody the change or vision you wish you to set forth or see actualized. There is a mighty power in using your body, in a literal and physical way, to cast your spell.

Materials

A shower

A pen (nontoxic, preferably)

Step into the shower and focus on cleansing your body and mind of the day's troubles, worries, to-dos, and excitement. Let it all wash away—down the drain, away from your mind, away from your body. Use the shower to create a space that is ready to hold your intention and energies.

After you're out of the shower, find a private space to close your eyes and focus on your intention. Use your pen to write it on a part of your body—it can be somewhere hidden or somewhere you can see it (so you think about it often). You might choose to write in the present tense:

I am abundant.
I am powerful.
I am loved.
I am light.
I take no shit.
I am resilient.
I am a boss.
I am worthy.
I am cared for.
I am healed.

Let the words sink into your skin over time—don't scrub them off!—joining in the engine of actualization that is your body.

A Collaborative Word Magic Ritual for Building Love and Trust

Building a bond of love and trust is so important for strengthening and layering a partnership. Do this ritual with a friend, a partner, or someone in your coven. In one of my partnerships, we performed the following ritual, and it was fun and empowering and plenty vulnerable—all things that served not only to deepen our bond but also to tap into a sense of collaborative magic. (We often practice magic alone, so it's a unique challenge to pool energies and powers together with someone else.)

For this ritual, you'll want to write short incantations for your partner and give them something to hold on to—a talisman of sorts—for three days. It's best to do this during the full moon, a time of intense power and receptivity.

Materials

A small piece of paper

A pen

A small talisman or token that represents your love and trust

Day 1: Sit with your partner. Ask them:

What do you want to manifest?

When they tell you, focus your energy and write a short, specific, and powerful incantation that you believe will help them manifest their intention. Have them do the same for you.

Next, smoke- or water-cleanse your talisman (see page 25) and program it to represent your love and loyalty to your partner. Trade these items and the incantations.

Days 2 and 3: Both of you should carry your talismans; each time you feel it in your pocket, think back on your partner's love and trust. Read their incantation aloud several times during the day, trusting that their words are meant to help you. Ask them to do the same for you.

Honing your sense of collaborative magic—as well as learning to trust that your partner cares for you—is an important (and magical) part of any relationship.

A Sand-and-Sea Spell
for Manifesting

The sea is a powerful symbol of magic—she is all-powerful, generous, life-giving, mysterious, enchanting, and kind. She is controlled by the moon and is a representation of the tides of life, how we ebb and flow, change and grow, pull back and rush forward. She is darkness and light at once.

If you are lucky enough to be near the sea, use the sea's energies to manifest your intention.

Materials

A beach

Make a trip to the beach into an opportunity for magic—simply by walking to the shoreline, where the sand becomes wet and receptive, and using your fingers to write out your request. I use the sea often for healing spells and transformation spells, pulling on its powers of change and purification.

Simply sit before your words and watch the ocean pull them into its blue world. Thank the water for its generosity, and if you can, bathe in it—connect with its vastness and imagine all the potential it represents.

A Diary Practice for
Seasonal Goals

The seasons inform so much about our health and well-being. Seasonal affective disorder, for example, can attack our happiness, squeezing out any sense of joy or hope we have during cold winter days. Even if you don't experience prolonged bouts of darkness or snow or see dramatic seasonal changes, you can still set quarterly goals.

To rise above seasonal highs and lows, I tap into the pros and cons of Earth's natural cycles by keeping a diary during the equinoxes and solstices. This simple diary practice can help you experience the best of each season, set seasonal goals, and track your moods.

Materials

A beautiful journal

Colored pencils

Divide your journal into four sections (one for each season or quarter).

Decorate each season's opening page(s). What does that season mean to you? It could represent a change in nature or a personal change you want to manifest.

When the beginning of each season arrives, make two lists. Include your quarterly goals and what you love about that season. Find something positive and connect with that—as opposed to being overwhelmed or burdened by the difficulties one season may bring.

Work nature magic into your daily routines. Scribble ideas so you can remember magical workings. Record your summery sea magic spells, or write down recipes for magical spiced wine during the fall.

Write down your moods throughout each season. How does spring affect you? Is winter a time of great manifestation and clarity?

Look back on each season as you move ahead; let your notes illuminate you. If spring made you feel energized and hopeful, envision ways to keep that momentum going in the months ahead.

Store your old journals and start new ones each year. They just might become an important part of your magical practice, connecting you back to nature and yourself.

LAST-MINUTE LIGHT

——

Magic for Bathroom Stalls, Crying Corners, and Emergencies

Because the foundation of all magic is intent and imagination, you don't need an arsenal of tools to cast a last-minute spell or bring a little oomph to a dark day.

As you already know, tools are helpful and sacred to many practitioners—but you are typically the main ingredient in anything you do.

This chapter prepares you for those unique circumstances when you don't have a candle or even a space to call your own. For when you need some magic but you're at work, in the middle of a crowded subway station, or at the doctor's office, clenching your jaw in worry.

It also offers "spell prep" ideas so you can create small magical bags or on-the-go tools to be kept in your bag or desk at work. You can use most of these items for the spells, rituals, and practices throughout this book as well as for any seat-of-your-pants spells you want to make on your own.

 The foundation of all magic is intent and imagination

Magic in a Pinch

Here are some of the ways you can make last-minute magic:

Mantras for Inspiration

Write out a handful of mantras that speak to you; they don't have to be fancy—something like "You're a badass" or "You're a queen" works. Keep them in a mantra box on your desk at work, on your bedside table, or near the front door, where you can pick one up as you leave each day. Pull a mantra every time you need a pick-me-up. Add to this any time, making it an ongoing ritual.

When You Need to Protect Your Energetic Field in Public

Imagine a white bubble surrounding your body. Pull it in on all sides and fill it with light so that you're glowing or glittering—and imagine that anyone passing by you can't get past that sparkling field encompassing your body. It's useful, for example, when you're in an agitated, crowded, potentially hostile public transportation station where energies are rabid.

Cleanse Yourself of Stress or Tension

Find a bowl of water or use a sink, and gently and mindfully wash your hands. Whisper:

Cleanse me, clear me, and guide me.

Seek Wisdom in Nature

Keep a plant on your desk, go outside to a nearby garden, or take a stroll through the park. Simply ask the earth for clarity. Listen to the trees, feel the greenery (even if it's a tiny houseplant!), or put your feet to the ground. Take a deep breath and let nature do her work.

Love Yourself

Take a moment to wrap your arms around yourself. Or simply stare lovingly into the mirror and say, "I love you. You are a badass. I am amazed by your accomplishments," or "Thank you for being you." You can also simply hold a rose quartz to your heart in an act of self-love when you're feeling especially down.

Remember: This is the most radical, magical act of all. Once you feel that love for yourself, your inner power as a person—and as a magical practitioner of any sort—will only grow.

Afternoon Power-Up for Busy Days

Sip your tea. Brew up a mug of your favorite herbal tea, infusing it with the intention of waking up, feeling energized, and powering through your day. Finish the entire cup. Herbal teas that pep the spirits include orange, lemon, peppermint, ginseng, and green tea.

Have a crystal handy. Keep a crystal at your work desk. Tourmaline and carnelian are both used to increase energy, though you can work with any crystal that speaks to you. Make sure to program it beforehand to be your power-up crystal. Hold it in your hand and close your eyes when you need a dose-up. (Don't forget to cleanse it energetically, with the moon, in water, or in salt.)

Get down to earth. Stand outside, feet on the ground, and take three deep breaths. Ask the earth to fill you with light and energy. If you are in a wheelchair or can't get outside, find a light source and simply ask the sun to fill you with energy. You can also find a water source, like a sink, and run your hands under the water, acknowledging the water's cool, generous flow.

Draw a sigil. Create a sigil (a magical symbol) that represents regeneration and energy. Keep it on a piece of paper under your stack of paperwork or computer, hang it at your desk, or even draw it on the inside of your wrist or hand. (Note: Some ink is toxic, so be aware of what you're using before you draw.)

SIGIL MAGIC

Have you ever been drawn to an image—a symbol or a shape? Have you ever found yourself always scribbling the same sort of image into your notebook? In a way, that's a sigil. Sigils are symbolic representations of your goals and intentions—and they can be used easily as a form of quick magic or incorporated into your ritual or spell-work.

Many practitioners first select a word of intention (confidence, love, money). Next, pull the letters (many witches pull only the consonants) from the word and draw them as overlapping shapes. Have fun with your sigil practice! Work the image so it hides the meaning of your original word and becomes a new symbol in itself. Once done, charge or program it with your goals, and leave it in a place of power (your wallet or your windowsill, for example). If you're curious, I created a sigil for love (see below). See if you can spot the letters entwined with one another.

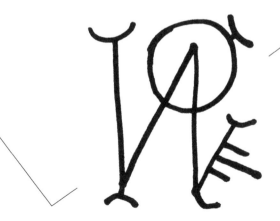

Create Your Own Traveling Magic Bag

Make your magic bag out of anything from a sachet bag (many Etsy and craft shops carry affordable velvet or organza bags) to a zip-lock baggie. You'll keep it on you for everyday purposes (e.g., going to and from work, heading to a friend's house), so find a size that feels right.

Select a few small items that make sense to you. Here are some that I carry, along with what I use them for:

- A drawing of a sigil (a symbolic representation of your goal or intent) that represents something important to you (see page 147)
- A small crystal of your choosing (crystals can be used to focus or tune energy around a specific emotion or goal)
- A programmed power lipstick (programmed lipsticks can help you feel powerful or confident when applied; see page 98)

- A vial of moon water. To make moon water, you can charge a lidded mason jar of water under the moon's direct light (or even at a window). You can carry this water on you in a vial if you need to dab some on your skin for a pick-me-up, or you can even make tea with it to infuse any elixir with the moon's powerful properties.
- A note of encouragement or love to yourself (these are just lovely, especially when you're feeling down—your word is your magic!)
- A tiny votive (because you never know when you'll want to cast a spell, do you?)
- A small bottle of blessed cleansing spray. To make your own cleansing spray, simply take a few drops of essential oil and mix it into a small spray bottle of water or even witch hazel. You can use this to cleanse your space, or program the spray bottle to get rid of negative energy.
- Your favorite calming tea (to meditate with or ground you while drinking)
- Yarn or thread for binding (tying a knot is a powerful method of binding)
- A small mirror (mirrors reflect back the energy they receive, so concentrate on feeling positive, confident, and receptive while using one)

Create Your Coven

Find like-minded people who are inclusive, creative, and interested in magic. Once you do, you can host "moon parlors" or "sun dates," little get-togethers that allow you to moon-bathe or sun-bathe together. Make socializing magical. Connecting with others, asking questions, sharing ideas, learning new things, and reading one another's energy lets you build your skills as a witch, an empath, and a friend. For more about modern covens, see below.

WHAT IS A COVEN?

A coven is a gathering or community of witches or magical practitioners. Historically, covens gather to practice ceremonial magic or to celebrate feasts or festivals. For example, Pagans, Wiccans, and other coven members come together to celebrate Imbolc—the arrival of spring— in ritual and feast. Today, the word *coven* may also be used in a less traditional way. A modern coven might be composed of witches, or those who identify with the archetype of the witch, who provide magical or emotional support to one another, help one another develop their magical or spiritual knowledge, or provide opportunities to work collaborative magic.

A coven might get together to work fashion magic by dressing up together and wearing power colors as a way to invoke magic and empowerment. Or they might gather to share new learnings about tarot, crystals, or dreamwork. Covens may also take the form of more public community groups—digital or in person—allowing more folks to take part, find support, and connect with other like-minded witches. *Luna Luna*, my magazine, offers a digital coven space on Facebook (facebook.com/groups/TheLuminousCommunity) for folks interested in magic, art, and community. Join us!

Word Witchery

There is an endless sum of magic in stating your intent and saying what you mean. It's not always easy, but using your words—with yourself or others—is about as empowering as it gets, especially in a culture where women and other marginalized groups are consistently silenced. Some magic phrases are:

- No
- I'm not interested
- I don't have time
- Please refer to me as she/he/they
- I am creative
- I am enough
- I am capable
- I don't want this
- This is temporary
- Let's collaborate
- That doesn't work for me, but this does . . .
- I need
- I want
- I am safe
- I have an idea
- Be inclusive
- Don't touch me
- Help
- I love you
- Thank you

FINDING YOUR CRAFT

From Sex Spellcraft to Kitchen
Witchery, Find the Kind of
Magic That Works for You

Everyone is beautifully and inherently different—and the same goes for people practicing magic. There is no one kind of practice, and no one right way to make magic. Some practitioners may be interested in working regularly with a coven while others may be drawn toward working specifically with herbs or glamour.

For so long, witches have been intuiting their magic. With this book, I focus very specifically on that innate and intuitive sense—working with what feels right as opposed to super-structured rituals, and using a few specific items, as opposed to spending money and time buying ingredients that might not necessarily feel natural. That intuitive magic is largely informed by your interests.

Everyday magic is the magic made in mundane tasks. It's the power of intention fused into your daily routines. It's the way your passions and energy make things happen. It's the way you move through the world, spreading compassion or building community or using your home to conjure good for your family or friends.

In this chapter, we'll discuss several ways to make everyday magic with . . .

- The earth
- Fashion and glamour
- Water
- Healing
- Community
- Home and hearth
- Sex

And remember, this chapter is just a starting point. You can (and should!) absolutely combine interests and strengths in your practice. Your practice will likely pivot and evolve as you grow too, so don't be beholden to any one kind of magic.

The Green Thumb:
Work with the Earth

The earth is itself magic—full of energy, in tune with the moon, and beautiful even in its death and rebirth—which is why working with it can be so fulfilling. If you find yourself more energized and recalibrated by a day at the beach or during a long walk surrounded by trees and plants, play with that in your practice.

There are plenty of ways to work with the earth, many of them simpler than you might think.

Work in your garden or a community garden. Spending time tending to a garden is a beautiful (and socially responsible) way to ground yourself and build your connection to nature. As you dig your fingers into the cool earth, think about its life-giving forces, and how it roots you to the bigger picture.

Grow herbs, like mint, lavender, or sage, in your home. According to lore, it's customary to make an offering to the earth as thanks when beginning a garden, even if it's a few pots at your windowsill. You can create a small ritual of any sort, but I like to offer up an item of meaning—perhaps a ring or small charm—to the earth, burying it in the soil.

Create a crystal grid. Crystal grids allow you to combine the energies of several crystals—for whatever your purpose is—in a geometric pattern. Choose a place for your grid, decide your intention for it, and lay out your specific crystals in a geometric shape. Be sure to have a center crystal. This is usually a stone with a point, so it can direct energy.

For billions of years, crystals have naturally formed all over the earth and underground. Many are formed in mineral-rich water, while others are formed in rock. Depending on temperature, pressure, and location, they grow in unique and varied sizes. Crystals are representations of the earth's creative energies. Simply holding a crystal or keeping one near you can help you tap into the earth. Creating a grid lets you focus on how each crystal represents a part of your intention.

Clothing Conjure:
Make Magic Fashion Statements

Plenty of witches work with fashion—their clothing, accessories, and even their makeup—to up the magical ante. Magic is all about intention; when we dress ourselves—choosing the colors and the fabrics and the mood of our outfit—we are making a statement and a choice that says, "This is the energy I will bring to the world." My magic of choice? Blood-red lips and a pair of heeled boots, along with a structured, long black blazer. It's a pretty Scorpio choice—all dark and sultry—and it says, "I am here."

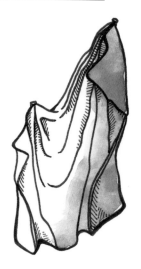

To use fashion magic, you can go in many directions—from what you wear to the fabrics around your home.

Wear colors that symbolize your mood. When you wake up each morning, create a statement outfit—especially on days where it counts (you're on a job interview, you're starting a new role, you're meeting a friend in need). It doesn't have to be fancy or expensive. You just need to appoint each item a meaning. Does your shirt make you feel powerful? Does wearing a specific color make you feel sensual, alive, or successful? Tap into that! Let the clothing do the magic as you go through your day. Turn getting dressed into a ritual:

- Light a candle and play some mood-boosting music while selecting your outfit.
- Decide what your intention is for each piece of clothing.
- State your intention while dressing and looking into the mirror.

Make a magical pillow. Choose fabric that speaks to you in some way, be it pink satin or black organza, for example. Cut it into two pieces, stuff it with goose down or fiberfill, slip a little note of intention or a crystal inside, and sew it closed. *Voilà!* You have a magical pillow working your intent.

Donate your clothes to a shelter or thrift store. Donating your clothes is a way to alleviate waste and spread the magic of generosity to your community. Before you donate your clothes, set an intention to them: that they might find the exact person who needs them and go a long way toward helping them. You can light a candle or cleanse the clothes with a bit of palo santo before sending them off so that they can be cleared of any old energy. Another potent way to work fashion magic is to rally a group of friends (or your coven!) to donate to local shelters. Community work can be a powerful thing. Combined energies are engines for change.

Mermaid Magic:
Work with Water

Water magic might be right for you if you feel especially connected to beaches, lakes, and rivers, and whenever you swim or bathe, you feel instantly recharged and energized. Working with water magic is one of the easiest and most powerful ways to connect with nature and develop your skills as a practitioner. (Hint: I'm a water witch! Water is my go-to in times of chaos and happiness.)

Take a magical bath. Intentional bathing is one of the most powerful things you can do magically. It not only cleanses you physically but it can also recalibrate your mind:

- Choose the reason for your bath. Is it to destress, prep for a ritual, meditate, or ground?
- Place associated crystals on the four corners of your bathtub to boost your intention.
- Use bath salts and essential oils to soothe your skin and senses.
- Close your eyes and envision the water cleansing you of all negative energies and filling you with cleansed, supportive energy.

Visit hot springs. In Chinese medicine, hot springs are known to boost well-being and general health. Essentially, a hot spring is a geothermally heated source of water that rises from the earth's crust. (Kind of like magic!) There are geothermal hot springs all over the world. Seek one out; they are a powerful way to connect with nature.

Cleanse your and your partner's hands. I once attended a powerful ritual at a place called Catland Books, a metaphysical shop here in Brooklyn, New York. The guide had my partner and I cleanse one another's hands in rose water (which is good for conjuring the energy of love, because many people associate roses with love and the heart) while looking each other in the eyes. It was incredibly powerful (if not uncomfortable, which was a good thing). My partner was another witch, so between the two of us, our energies were fully activated.

You can do this by yourself or with a partner:

- Fill a large wooden bowl with lukewarm water.
- Cleanse the water with smoke from palo santo or cedar.
- Add a few drops of rose oil or another essential oil, or even a few rose petals.
- Slowly wash your hands—and your partner's hands, if you're working with one—in the water, focusing on sending love and compassion through your touch.

Gather sea water in a spray bottle. The ocean is a tremendous and powerful being—she is guided by the moon's cycles and is both capable of great destruction and creating and sustaining life. If you can get to an ocean, bottle some sea water in a spray bottle. Use it to power up spells by simply spraying it on the base of your candle during a spell—especially if you're a water sign—or spraying it on yourself to conjure the ocean's power and grace.

The Healing Touch:
Magical Support

You may feel that healing is your call—to lend others support, to lift others up, and to treat wounds or traumas. There are many ways to hone in on healing.

Work with empathy and compassion. Entering into magical workings with an empathic mind-set may be difficult—we are human, but doing so can be a powerful tool for change and growth. As a healer, you'll want to hone your empathy and compassion by sending it out into your community and the world. You can do this in physical and magical ways—by exercising empathy when times are rough and anger or division feels more natural, and by envisioning compassionate, sparkling light surrounding people when they need it most. (Just be sure to give yourself time to recuperate energy. Healing yourself and recharging is always key.)

Create healing herbal tinctures. Along with seeing a healthcare provider you trust, you can use at-home herbal tinctures to soothe aches and promote healing. (Check with your doc first.) Tinctures are used orally and made with the leaves or flowers of certain plants.

Work with healing crystals and stones. Here are some great options:

- Hematite: promotes relief from anxiety, stabilizes emotions
- Amethyst: deepens intuition and awareness of traumas and memories
- Obsidian: helps make holistic life changes
- Moonstone: supports humanitarian efforts and spreads love
- Rose quartz: promotes receptivity to love and sends love to others

Kitchen Witchery:
Conjure through Cooking

Kitchen witchery can involve creating yummy confections or powerful elixirs, or creating magic within the home in general. It's focused largely on easy, everyday tasks as simple as whipping up a soup, doing chores, or prepping the home for each new season.

Cleanse and purify your space with natural goods. Try these options:

- Add essential oils to the water you use to mop your floors or clean surfaces. A home that smells of lavender is peaceful and serene.
- Burn sage or palo santo to cleanse the space before family arrives or after a group leaves.
- Use your besom to sweep out old, toxic, negative energies— or to renew your home before the change of each season (see the Besom-Building Practice on page 65).

Brew tea with intention. While making tea, set it with an intention— to be manifested once the tea is finished.

Charge ingredients under the moon. Leave nonperishable ingredients out in the moonlight to power them up and fill them with magical intention. You can also put out your cooking utensils.

Eat with mindfulness. Thanking the earth for your food—and uttering a line of gratitude before each meal—is key in kitchen witchery. Enjoy your food slowly and with intention.

Spring-clean. Turn your spring-cleaning into a ritual to recharge and energize your home. Start by lighting a candle and burning some sage or palo santo, and intentionally remove unwanted items or clear out winter wear. Welcome in new, cleansed energy, ready to reap abundance, health, and happiness.

Practice apartment magic. If you live in a tiny apartment, you can still perform kitchen witchery. Double up on uses for your space. Use a kitchen window to grow herbs. If you have a windowsill, use it as an altar for candles, oils, and homemade sprays.

Community Conjurer:
Use the Power of Combined Energies

Maybe your craft doesn't always include power objects or tarot cards or crystals. Maybe your craft isn't solitary. Your inner witch may thrive on the way you exist and interact with others. It could be that you prefer to encourage, support, and protect your community, or maybe you have a knack for bringing people together with a shared goal (like a coven). Community witchery is a great way to use the magic of people to get things done.

Assemble a group to resist acts of social injustice. Witchcraft goes hand in hand with social justice. While many think of magic as casting spells alone in your bedroom, it's more than that. Witches—and those who have practiced magic in any way—have been persecuted for years. There are still stigmas, fears, and punishments exacted on witches the world over. This is why it's important, as beings of love and light, to support others, especially marginalized people, who need it.

Run a community coven meetup. While many people practice magic in solitude, it can be empowering to find other like-minded folks who want to talk about their practices and ideas. Organize a meetup once a month or on the equinoxes to come together and get to know one another. This could take the form of a ritual focused around an intention (like welcoming winter or healing a community issue) or a potluck feast.

Organize a magical panel. Collect some of your favorite witches—or even local authors who write about magic—to get together and discuss their work or ideas. You can ask questions or facilitate a Q&A. Not only will you get to meet folks with similar interests, but you can also kick off the event with a short ritual or collaborative spell.

Sex Magic:
Harness Erotic Energies for Manifesting

According to witch and editor of *Slutist*, Kristen Sollée (who wrote the foreword to this book), this oh-so-potent form of magic is simply about using your own sexual energy (like during masturbation) to manifest intent.

Put simply, sex magic isn't about being sexy or wearing lingerie or having sex while surrounded by dripping red candles (although melodrama is always welcome). It's about taking that natural energy inside of you and using it to fuel your magic.

Masturbate under the full moon. When the moon is in its most powerful phase, harness it. Crawl under your covers, spritz on a bit of your favorite perfume or essential oil, and use your body for your manifestation magic. When you reach orgasm (or your mental peak during this self-love time), simply state your intent out loud or think it clearly in your head. That energy is real and intense and raw—and when cast, it gets sent out into the universe as a resounding "boom."

Visualize a sigil. Create a sigil that represents a goal or desire—it might represent success or opportunity or inspire self-esteem. While masturbating, keep the sigil emblazoned in your mind. You can also draw it on your hand or somewhere on your body to fuel your energy with its powers.

Meditate on a mantra. This can be done by yourself or with a partner.

- By yourself: Close your eyes and repeat a mantra to yourself as you masturbate. Choose a simple, single line and focus on it and your breath as you masturbate. This can be an intense experience, so be sure to set aside some alone time to really experience it. Keep that mantra in your mind as you finish.

- With a partner: Agree on a mantra or meditative vision with your partner. You may both keep it in mind as you have sex, focusing on it together as you near the finish. In this practice, you'll manifest double the energy—working toward a goal as a union of energies.

Conclusion

As we come to an end, there is one resounding truth: No matter what you believe, or what your dreams and goals are, true magic is found in your intent. It's not always easy—nor is it always beautiful, immediately transformative, or cinematic—but deciding every passing day, in some small way, that you are valuable and powerful, is magic in itself. With this book, I hope you walk away with a ritual of self, with an altar designed to see your way through the fog, and with written words that speak a greater truth. In the great expanse of life, all we can hope for is to inhabit the good and make space for it. Magic is what happens when we try for that, bit by bit, each day. Thank you for making space for ritual, for self-reflection, and for play.

Resources

Books

Crystals

Crystal Healing and Sacred Pleasure by Vanessa Cuccia

The Crystal Bible by Judy Hall

Inner Magic and Personal Development

Codependent No More by Melody Beattie

Creative Visualization: Use the Power of Your Imagination to Create What You Want In Your Life by Shakti Gawain

Forest Bathing: How Trees Can Help You Find Health and Happiness by Dr. Qing Li

Jailbreaking the Goddess by Lasara Firefox Allen

Meeting the Shadow: The Hidden Power of the Dark Side of Human Nature by Connie Zweig

Women Who Run with the Wolves: Myths and Stories of the Wild Woman Archetype by Clarissa Pinkola Estés, Ph.D.

Literature

A Burst of Light and Other Essays by Audre Lorde

Literary Witches by Taisia Kitaiskaia

The Diary of Anaïs Nin by Anaïs Nin

The House of the Spirits by Isabel Allende

Witchcraft, Magic, and Mythology

A Witches' Bible: The Complete Witches' Handbook by Janet and Stewart Farrar

Compendium Maleficarum by Francesco Maria Guazzo

Egyptian Mythology A to Z by Pat Remler

Grovedaughter Witchery: Practical Spellcraft by Bree NicGarran

Linda Goodman's Sun Signs by Linda Goodman

Death

Podcasts

The Witch Wave
witchwavepodcast.com

The Fat Feminist Witch
fatfeministwitch.podbean.com

Serpent Cast
theserpentcast.tumblr.com

Tarot for the Wild Soul
lindsaymack.com/podcast

Modern Witch
modernwitch.podbean.com

HiPPie Witch
joannadevoe.com/p/
hippie-witch-radio

New World Witchery
newworldwitchery.com/
category/podcast

Websites

The Hoodwitch
HoodWitch.com

HausWitch
Hauswitch.com

Stay Connected

Luna Luna Magazine
LunaLunaMagazine.com
@lunalunamag
#lunalunamag

Light Magic for Dark Times
LightMagicDarkTimes.com
#LightMagicDarkTimes

Lisa Marie Basile
lisamariebasile.com

Acknowledgments

For my mother, whose resilience and survival planted the seeds for this book. For my late grandmother Dorothy, who held me up when I was lost. For my brother David, who supports me no matter what. For Benjamin, who is the light of my life.

For all the magic makers, dreamers, writers, editors, fighters, survivors, and creators at Luna Luna Magazine and in our community. Thank you for being a force for good in this world. There are too many to list, so please just read our whole website: www.lunalunamagazine.com

For the many, many magazine editors, literary agents, writers, reading series hosts, podcast creators and press editors who have taken a chance on my work and who let me turn my stories and poems into magic. For the poets who have read alongside me. For the witches who have adorned my life in light. For the people who have helped me explore my dark.

For all the local witchcraft/occult shops that work hard to bring magic, activism, and education to their communities.

For the educators, foster parents and supporters who got me through foster care.

For my incredible editor at Quarto, Jess Haberman—who took a chance on me. For the dedicated Lydia Anderson, Meredith Quinn, and Erika Heilman. To Kristen J. Sollee, for your support here.

For everyone who has had to rebuild, recreate and reimagine. For everyone who lives with a small sadness that must be regularly tended to. For those who have experienced grief and loss. For those who believe in the ritual of regeneration. For the silenced, the marginalized, and the invisible. For those of you who rebel against the status quo. For those of you who wade through the dark. For my friend, the light.

For those of you right here, right now, reading this.

About the Author

Lisa Marie Basile is a poet-witch and founding creative director of *Luna Luna* magazine—a diary of darkness and light, literature, identity, and magic. Her work encounters the intersection of ritual and wellness, chronic illness, magic, overcoming trauma, and poetry. She is the author of poetry collections *Andalucia* and *Apocryphal*, as well as the forthcoming *Nympholepsy*. She has written for the *New York Times*, Narratively, *Grimoire* magazine, Venefica, The Establishment, Refinery29, Bust, Hello Giggles, and more. Her work has been nominated for the *Best American Experimental Writing* anthology and for several Pushcart Prizes, and has appeared in *The Best Small Fictions*, selected by Pulitzer Prize–winning writer Robert Olen Butler. Lisa Marie earned a master's degree in writing from The New School and studied literature and psychology at Pace University. She lives in New York City.

Index